P9-ARZ-643

IRAQ

OPPOSING VIEWPOINTS®

IRAQ

OPPOSING VIEWPOINTS®

Other Books of Related Interest

IRAQ

OPPOSING VIEWPOINTS®

William Dudley, *Book Editor*

Daniel Leone, *President*
Bonnie Szumski, *Publisher*
Scott Barbour, *Managing Editor*
Helen Cothran, *Senior Editor*

OPPOSING
VIEWPOINTS®
SERIES

GREENHAVEN
PRESS®

THOMSON
————*————
GALE

San Diego • Detroit • New York • San Francisco • Cleveland
New Haven, Conn. • Waterville, Maine • London • Munich

LIBRARY OF CONGRESS CATALOGING-IN-PUBLICATION DATA

Iraq : opposing viewpoints / William Dudley, book editor.
   p. cm. — (Opposing viewpoints series)
  Includes bibliographical references and index.
  ISBN 0-7377-2286-X (lib. : alk. paper) — ISBN 0-7377-2287-8 (pbk. : alk. paper)
    1. Iraq War, 2003—Causes. 2. Iraq War, 2003—Moral and ethical
aspects—United States. 3. United States relations—Iraq. 4. Iraq relations—
United States. 5. United States—Foreign relations—2001– . 6. Democracy—Iraq.
I. Dudley, William. II. Opposing viewpoints series (Unnumbered)
DS79.76.I726 2004
956.7044'3—dc22   2003049374

Printed in the United States of America

"Congress shall make
no law. . . abridging the
freedom of speech, or of
the press."

First Amendment to the U.S. Constitution

The basic foundation of our democracy is the First
Amendment guarantee of freedom of expression.
The Opposing Viewpoints Series is dedicated to the
concept of this basic freedom and the idea that it is
more important to practice it than to enshrine it.

Contents

Why Consider Opposing Viewpoints?

"The only way in which a human being can make some approach to knowing the whole of a subject is by hearing what can be said about it by persons of every variety of opinion and studying all modes in which it can be looked at by every character of mind. No wise man ever acquired his wisdom in any mode but this."

John Stuart Mill

In our media-intensive culture it is not difficult to find differing opinions. Thousands of newspapers and magazines and dozens of radio and television talk shows resound with differing points of view. The difficulty lies in deciding which opinion to agree with and which "experts" seem the most credible. The more inundated we become with differing opinions and claims, the more essential it is to hone critical reading and thinking skills to evaluate these ideas. Opposing Viewpoints books address this problem directly by presenting stimulating debates that can be used to enhance and teach these skills. The varied opinions contained in each book examine many different aspects of a single issue. While examining these conveniently edited opposing views, readers can develop critical thinking skills such as the ability to compare and contrast authors' credibility, facts, argumentation styles, use of persuasive techniques, and other stylistic tools. In short, the Opposing Viewpoints Series is an ideal way to attain the higher-level thinking and reading skills so essential in a culture of diverse and contradictory opinions.

In addition to providing a tool for critical thinking, Opposing Viewpoints books challenge readers to question their own strongly held opinions and assumptions. Most people form their opinions on the basis of upbringing, peer pressure, and personal, cultural, or professional bias. By reading carefully balanced opposing views, readers must directly confront new ideas as well as the opinions of those with whom they disagree. This is not to simplistically argue that everyone who reads opposing views will—or should—change his or her opinion. Instead, the series enhances readers' understanding of their own views by encouraging confrontation with opposing ideas. Careful examination of others' views can lead to the readers' understanding of the logical inconsistencies in their own opinions, perspective on why they hold an opinion, and the consideration of the possibility that their opinion requires further evaluation.

Evaluating Other Opinions

To ensure that this type of examination occurs, Opposing Viewpoints books present all types of opinions. Prominent spokespeople on different sides of each issue as well as well-known professionals from many disciplines challenge the reader. An additional goal of the series is to provide a forum for other, less known, or even unpopular viewpoints. The opinion of an ordinary person who has had to make the decision to cut off life support from a terminally ill relative, for example, may be just as valuable and provide just as much insight as a medical ethicist's professional opinion. The editors have two additional purposes in including these less known views. One, the editors encourage readers to respect others' opinions—even when not enhanced by professional credibility. It is only by reading or listening to and objectively evaluating others' ideas that one can determine whether they are worthy of consideration. Two, the inclusion of such viewpoints encourages the important critical thinking skill of objectively evaluating an author's credentials and bias. This evaluation will illuminate an author's reasons for taking a particular stance on an issue and will aid in readers' evaluation of the author's ideas.

It is our hope that these books will give readers a deeper understanding of the issues debated and an appreciation of the complexity of even seemingly simple issues when good and honest people disagree. This awareness is particularly important in a democratic society such as ours in which people enter into public debate to determine the common good. Those with whom one disagrees should not be regarded as enemies but rather as people whose views deserve careful examination and may shed light on one's own.

Thomas Jefferson once said that "difference of opinion leads to inquiry, and inquiry to truth." Jefferson, a broadly educated man, argued that "if a nation expects to be ignorant and free . . . it expects what never was and never will be." As individuals and as a nation, it is imperative that we consider the opinions of others and examine them with skill and discernment. The Opposing Viewpoints Series is intended to help readers achieve this goal.

David L. Bender and Bruno Leone,
Founders

Greenhaven Press anthologies primarily consist of previously published material taken from a variety of sources, including periodicals, books, scholarly journals, newspapers, government documents, and position papers from private and public organizations. These original sources are often edited for length and to ensure their accessibility for a young adult audience. The anthology editors also change the original titles of these works in order to clearly present the main thesis of each viewpoint and to explicitly indicate the opinion presented in the viewpoint. These alterations are made in consideration of both the reading and comprehension levels of a young adult audience. Every effort is made to ensure that Greenhaven Press accurately reflects the original intent of the authors included in this anthology.

Introduction

"The nations in our coalition are determined to help the Iraqi people recover from years of tyranny. And we are determined to help build a free, and sovereign, and democratic nation."

President George W. Bush, July 23, 2003

On April 9, 2003, much of the world's attention was riveted on a scene in a public square in Baghdad, the capital city of the Middle Eastern nation of Iraq. Television cameras broadcast a picture of a group of Iraqi citizens, who, after several hours of trying and with the assistance of American soldiers and tanks, finally succeeded in toppling an enormous statue of Iraq's now-deposed leader, Saddam Hussein. For Americans watching on television, the fall of the statue marked the triumphal moment of a military campaign begun a few weeks earlier to remove a regime that was seen as a threat to American security. For the Iraqi people, the event marked the symbolic overthrow of a tyrannical ruler who had terrorized the nation for more than two decades. However, Saddam Hussein's political career—including its ignominious end—left several significant legacies that will make the rehabilitation of Iraq problematic.

Saddam Hussein joined the Baath Party, a political organization that preached Arab unity, nationalism, and revolution, while in college. By 1968, the Baath Party had taken over Iraq, and Hussein became the second-most important man in the Iraqi government behind President Ahmed Hassan al-Bakr. In 1979 Hussein replaced al-Bakr as president and immediately executed twenty-one high government officials he suspected of treason. It was but one of many actions that left Iraq with a legacy of brutal political oppression. Political opponents of Hussein were routinely tortured and jailed. Key government and security apparatus positions were parceled out to relatives and trusted members of Hussein's hometown and tribe. According to Middle East scholar Alon Ben-Meir, this combination of oppression and favoritism has left many Iraqis, even after Hussein's demise, "embittered, disillusioned, cynical, suspicious, and impatient." These traits of the Iraqi people will make it more difficult to create a functioning representative government in Iraq—a major policy objective of the United States.

Hussein's rule proved especially destructive to two of Iraq's three main ethnic and religious groups: Shiite Muslim Arabs and ethnic Kurds (Hussein was a Sunni Muslim Arab, a group that despite its minority status had historically held political power in Iraq). The "Anfal" campaign Hussein instigated to suppress the Kurds in the late 1980s was not the first time ethnic conflict had raged between Kurds and Arabs but it was the most ruthless. Iraqi forces destroyed thousands of Kurdish villages and killed more than one hundred thousand people, including five thousand from a 1988 chemical weapons attack on the Kurdish city of Halabja. Hussein also took extreme measures to keep Shiite Muslims under political control, ordering his troops to shoot and kill thousands when Shiites attempted an uprising in 1991. Saddam's actions may have kept Iraq from breaking apart into separate countries but at a terrible cost. The hostility between the nation's ethnic factions further complicates the establishment of a unified and democratic Iraq after Hussein's demise.

In addition to years of political and ethnic oppression, another legacy of Hussein's rule is a series of foreign policy misadventures that led to Iraqi defeats, years of diplomatic isolation and international sanctions, and ultimately foreign occupation. His decision to attack Iran in 1980 resulted in a eight-year war and stalemate that cost hundreds of thousands of Iraqi lives and left Iraq's economy in critical shape. His 1990 decision to invade Kuwait resulted in condemnation by the United Nations Security Council, international economic sanctions, and military defeat in 1991 at the hands of a large international force, led by the United States and including Saudi Arabia and other Arab nations.

Much of Iraq's urban infrastructure, including irrigation and water systems, was destroyed by American bombs during the 1991 conflict and was not replaced. Iraq's postwar rebuilding was hampered by the continuation of UN sanctions, which were to be lifted only when Iraq satisfactorily fulfilled UN demands that it verifiably relinquish all of its chemical, biological, and nuclear weapons, and halt all of its weapons of mass destruction programs. Although Hussein agreed to these conditions at the time of the 1991 cease-fire, he continued to obstruct efforts by the United Nations to inspect weapons sites. In 1998 inspectors from the UN Special Commission and the International Atomic Energy Agency were withdrawn from Iraq after Hussein reneged on promises of cooperation. Although seven hundred tons of chemical agents and other components of weapons of mass destruction programs had been found and destroyed, questions persisted about Iraq's remaining WMD capabilities. Hussein's refusal to fully cooperate with the United Nations meant that the last twelve years of his reign were marred by economic sanctions that severely hampered Iraq's economy and deprived Iraq's people of medicines, food, and clean water.

UN weapons inspections were given a final chance in late 2002, after the United Nations, at America's urging, passed a resolution calling for Iraq to demonstrate proof of disarmament or face military consequences. Iraq admitted a new team of UN weapons inspectors in November 2002. However, chief inspector Hans Blix reported in February 2002 that while no actual weapons of mass destruction had been uncovered, Iraq still was not fully cooperating in answering questions regarding its weapons programs. President George W. Bush cited Iraq's noncooperation and the potential threat that Iraq's weapons could pose to the United States as reasons for his decision in March 2003 to order American military forces into Iraq. A few weeks later Hussein's reign over Iraq was over.

While television news coverage that day in April showed Iraqis celebrating the end of Hussein's rule, the toppling of Saddam's statue did not signify the end of problems for Iraq and its people. Months after President Bush proclaimed the end of major combat operations in Iraq on May 1, 2003, the United States continued to station 150,000 soldiers in Iraq—a deployment that some people predict may last for years. Iraq also was experiencing guerrilla conflict and terrorist attacks—events that some people blamed on loyalists to Hussein's regime; some speculated that Hussein, whose whereabouts remained unknown months after his regime was deposed, was continuing to organize resistance to impede efforts by the United States to provide security for Iraq's people and install a new Iraqi government. These problems, as well as others Hussein had left in his wake, figure prominently in the ongoing debates that Iraqis, Americans, and members of the international community hold regarding the best way to help Iraq. Many of these problems are discussed in the following chapters of *Iraq: Opposing Viewpoints:* Was the 2003 War on Iraq Justified? What Role Should the United States Play in Iraq? What Kind of Government Should Iraq Have? What Lies in the Future for Iraq? Regardless of Hussein's personal fate, his adverse political legacy continues to affect the lives of Iraq's people and make the rehabilitation of Iraq after the war more difficult.

CHAPTER 1

Was the 2003 War on Iraq Justified?

Chapter Preface

The 2003 Iraq War lasted less than three weeks. It began in the early morning hours of March 20, when American missiles struck Baghdad. By April 9, U.S. forces had advanced into Baghdad. By April 15 Iraqi leader Saddam Hussein had vanished, and U.S. and allied officials pronounced the end of major combat operations. President George W. Bush repeated that pronouncement in a May 1 speech.

Although the war itself was short, arguments over whether it was justified had been made for months and years prior to the March 20 attacks—and continued long after the war was over. The roots of the crisis that led to the war go back at least as far as 1990, when George H.W. Bush was president and Iraq invaded and occupied its neighbor Kuwait. In the 1991 Persian Gulf War, Iraqi forces were driven from Kuwait by a United Nations coalition led by the United States. The war stopped short of removing Saddam Hussein from power, however.

Over the next decade Hussein continually blocked implementation of peace terms he had agreed to in 1991, which included pledges to destroy any chemical, nuclear, and biological weapons in Iraq. UN weapons inspectors were able to uncover some evidence of a nuclear weapons program and to find and destroy some chemical and biological weapons, but were frustrated by Hussein's efforts to make inspections difficult. Iraq's noncompliance led the UN to impose economic sanctions on the nation until Hussein proved willing to cooperate. During President Bill Clinton's tenure from 1993 to 2001, the United States maintained support for these sanctions and launched several military bombing strikes against Iraq in response to provocative acts, such as a 1993 attempted assassination of the former president Bush.

The administration of President George W. Bush (the former president's son) at first continued Clinton's policy of economic sanctions and occasional military strikes. However, in the wake of the September 11, 2001, terrorist attacks, the United States began to pursue a more aggressive policy toward Iraq as part of its broader war against terrorism. Administration officials charged Iraq with hiding weapons of mass destruction and cooperating with terrorist groups, and they openly spoke of the need for "regime change" to remove the threat posed by Saddam Hussein. In November 2002 the United Nations, at America's urging, passed a resolution calling for Iraq to demonstrate proof of disarmament to international inspectors or face "serious consequences." Iraq admitted a new team of UN weapons inspectors, but chief inspector Hans Blix later reported that while no actual weapons of mass destruction had been uncovered, Iraq had yet to fully cooperate in answering questions regarding its weapons programs. Some member nations of the UN Security Council, including France and Russia, argued that weapons inspections needed to be given more time and that Iraq did not pose an imminent threat to world security. However, American and British leaders disagreed and asserted that Iraq, by refusing to fully comply with UN resolutions, did pose a serious security threat. They also raised the possibility that Hussein might share such weapons with terrorists such as those who perpetrated the September 11 attacks. Citing the need to defend themselves from such a threat, a coalition of nations led by the United States and Great Britain attacked Iraq in March 2003.

The 2003 war resulted in a resounding victory for America and its allies. Indeed, the regime of Saddam Hussein was quickly dispatched. Questions and concerns regarding weapons of mass destruction did not go away so easily, however, and only intensified when American forces failed to find expected weapons stockpiles and facilities in the months following the war. The failure to find weapons of mass destruction has given some people pause. Military author and columnist Mark Bowden asserted in a May 25, 2003, column that if no weapons are found, he had to conclude that the American people "were led to war under false pretenses." Other observers, however, considered the end of Hussein's tyrannical regime to be justification enough. "As far as I'm concerned," wrote columnist Thomas Friedman, "we do not need to find any weapons of mass destruction to justify this war. . . . In ending Saddam's tyranny, a huge human engine for mass destruction has been broken." The viewpoints in this chapter continue the debate over Iraq's weapons of mass destruction and present other arguments for and against America's decision to invade Iraq in 2003.

"The security of the world requires disarming Saddam Hussein now."

An American Attack on Iraq Is Justified

George W. Bush

The following viewpoint is excerpted from President George W. Bush's address to the American people on March 17, 2003, in which he argues that diplomatic efforts to re-solve the Iraq crisis have failed and that military action may be necessary to overthrow Saddam Hussein's regime. He maintains that the United States has the right to defend it-self from regimes such as Hussein's that pose a clear security threat. According to the president, Hussein possesses weapons of mass destruction and has connections with in-ternational terrorists. He asserts that America tried to work with the United Nations to disarm Iraq without war, but Hussein's persistent defiance has left the United States with little choice but to resort to military action. Bush's speech also includes passages directed at the Iraqi people in which he states that an American-led attack will bring them libera-tion from tyranny. Hussein refused Bush's ultimatum that he leave Iraq; his regime was toppled by American-led military action several weeks later.

As you read, consider the following questions:

1. What dangers does Iraq pose to the United States, according to Bush?
2. Why have United Nations inspections failed to disarm Iraq, in the author's opinion?
3. What goals does the United States have for Iraq and the Middle East?

George W. Bush, address to the American people, Washington, DC, March 17, 2003.

My fellow citizens, events in Iraq have now reached the final days of decision. For more than a decade, the United States and other nations have pursued patient and honorable efforts to disarm the Iraqi regime without war. That regime pledged to reveal and destroy all its weapons of mass destruction as a condition for ending the Persian Gulf War in 1991.

Since then, the world has engaged in 12 years of diplomacy. We have passed more than a dozen resolutions in the United Nations Security Council. We have sent hundreds of weapons inspectors to oversee the disarmament of Iraq. Our good faith has not been returned.

The Iraqi regime has used diplomacy as a ploy to gain time and advantage. It has uniformly defied Security Council resolutions demanding full disarmament. Over the years, U.N. weapons inspectors have been threatened by Iraqi officials, electronically bugged, and systematically deceived. Peaceful efforts to disarm the Iraqi regime have failed again and again—because we are not dealing with peaceful men.

The Threat of Weapons of Mass Destruction

Intelligence gathered by this and other governments leaves no doubt that the Iraqi regime continues to possess and conceal some of the most lethal weapons ever devised. This regime has already used weapons of mass destruction against Iraq's neighbors and against Iraq's people.

The regime has a history of reckless aggression in the Middle East. It has a deep hatred of America and our friends. And it has aided, trained and harbored terrorists, including operatives of al Qaeda [the terrorist network responsible for the September 11, 2001, terrorist attacks].

The danger is clear: using chemical, biological or, one day, nuclear weapons, obtained with the help of Iraq, the terrorists could fulfill their stated ambitions and kill thousands or hundreds of thousands of innocent people in our country, or any other.

The United States and other nations did nothing to deserve or invite this threat. But we will do everything to defeat it. Instead of drifting along toward tragedy, we will set a course toward safety. Before the day of horror can come, before it is too late to act, this danger will be removed.

The United States of America has the sovereign authority to use force in assuring its own national security. That duty falls to me, as Commander-in-Chief, by the oath I have sworn, by the oath I will keep.

Attempts to Work with the United Nations

Recognizing the threat to our country, the United States Congress voted overwhelmingly last year [2002] to support the use of force against Iraq. America tried to work with the United Nations to address this threat because we wanted to resolve the issue peacefully. We believe in the mission of the United Nations. One reason the U.N. was founded after the second world war was to confront aggressive dictators, actively and early, before they can attack the innocent and destroy the peace.

An Important Decision

At a . . . fundamental level, the failure to remove Saddam [Hussein] would mean that, despite [the terrorist attacks] on September 11 [2001], we as a nation are still unwilling to shoulder the responsibilities of global leadership, even to protect ourselves. If we turn away from the Iraq challenge—because we fear the use of ground troops, because we don't want the job of putting Iraq back together afterwards, because we would prefer not to be deeply involved in a messy part of the world—then we will have made a momentous and fateful decision. We do not expect President [George W.] Bush to make that choice. We expect the president will courageously decide to destroy Saddam's regime. No step would contribute more toward shaping a world order in which our people and our liberal civilization can survive and flourish.

Robert Kagan and William Kristol, *Weekly Standard*, January 21, 2002.

In the case of Iraq, the Security Council did act, in the early 1990s. Under Resolutions 678 and 687—both still in effect—the United States and our allies are authorized to use force in ridding Iraq of weapons of mass destruction. This is not a question of authority, it is a question of will.

Last September [2002], I went to the U.N. General Assembly and urged the nations of the world to unite and bring an end to this danger. On November 8th, the Security Council unanimously passed Resolution 1441, finding Iraq in material breach of its obligations, and vowing serious consequences if Iraq did not fully and immediately disarm.

Today [March 17, 2003], no nation can possibly claim that Iraq has disarmed. And it will not disarm so long as Saddam Hussein holds power. For the last four-and-a-half months, the United States and our allies have worked within the Security Council to enforce that Council's long-standing demands. Yet, some permanent members of the Security Council have publicly announced they will veto any resolution that compels the disarmament of Iraq. These governments share our assessment of the danger, but not our resolve to meet it. Many nations, however, do have the resolve and fortitude to act against this threat to peace, and a broad coalition is now gathering to enforce the just demands of the world. The United Nations Security Council has not lived up to its responsibilities, so we will rise to ours.

In recent days [in February and March 2003], some governments in the Middle East have been doing their part. They have delivered public and private messages urging the dictator to leave Iraq, so that disarmament can proceed peacefully. He has thus far refused. All the decades of deceit and cruelty have now reached an end. Saddam Hussein and his sons must leave Iraq within 48 hours. Their refusal to do so will result in military conflict, commenced at a time of our choosing. For their own safety, all foreign nationals—including journalists and inspectors—should leave Iraq immediately.

A Message for Iraqis

Many Iraqis can hear me tonight in a translated radio broadcast, and I have a message for them. If we must begin a military campaign, it will be directed against the lawless men who rule your country and not against you. As our coalition takes away their power, we will deliver the food and medicine you need. We will tear down the apparatus of terror and we will help you to build a new Iraq that is prosperous and free. In a free Iraq, there will be no more wars of aggression against your neighbors, no more poison factories, no more executions of dissidents, no more torture chambers and rape rooms. The tyrant will soon be gone. The day of your liberation is near.

It is too late for Saddam Hussein to remain in power. It is not too late for the Iraqi military to act with honor and protect your country by permitting the peaceful entry of coalition forces to eliminate weapons of mass destruction. Our forces will give Iraqi military units clear instructions on actions they can take to avoid being attacked and destroyed. I urge every member of the Iraqi military and intelligence services, if war comes, do not fight for a dying regime that is not worth your own life. . . .

Should Saddam Hussein choose confrontation, the American people can know that every measure has been taken to avoid war, and every measure will be taken to win it. Americans understand the costs of conflict because we have paid them in the past. War has no certainty, except the certainty of sacrifice.

The Terrorist Threat

Yet, the only way to reduce the harm and duration of war is to apply the full force and might of our military, and we are prepared to do so. If Saddam Hussein attempts to cling to power, he will remain a deadly foe until the end. In desperation, he and terrorists groups might try to conduct terrorist operations against the American people and our friends. These attacks are not inevitable. They are, however, possible. And this very fact underscores the reason we cannot live under the threat of blackmail. The terrorist threat to America and the world will be diminished the moment that Saddam Hussein is disarmed. . . .

Our government is on heightened watch against these dangers. Just as we are preparing to ensure victory in Iraq, we are taking further actions to protect our homeland.

The Risks of Inaction

We are now acting because the risks of inaction would be far greater. In one year, or five years, the power of Iraq to inflict harm on all free nations would be multiplied many times over. With these capabilities, Saddam Hussein and his terrorist allies could choose the moment of deadly conflict when they are strongest. We choose to meet that threat now, where it arises, before it can appear suddenly in our skies and cities.

The cause of peace requires all free nations to recognize new and undeniable realities. In the 20th century, some chose to appease murderous dictators, whose threats were allowed to grow into genocide and global war. In this century, when evil men plot chemical, biological and nuclear terror, a policy of appeasement could bring destruction of a kind never before seen on this earth.

Terrorists and terror states do not reveal these threats with fair notice, in formal declarations—and responding to such enemies only after they have struck first is not self-defense, it is suicide. The security of the world requires disarming Saddam Hussein now.

As we enforce the just demands of the world, we will also honor the deepest commitments of our country. Unlike Saddam Hussein, we believe the Iraqi people are deserving and capable of human liberty. And when the dictator has departed, they can set an example to all the Middle East of a vital and peaceful and self-governing nation.

The United States, with other countries, will work to advance liberty and peace in that region. Our goal will not be achieved overnight, but it can come over time. The power and appeal of human liberty is felt in every life and every land. And the greatest power of freedom is to overcome hatred and violence, and turn the creative gifts of men and women to the pursuits of peace.

That is the future we choose. Free nations have a duty to defend our people by uniting against the violent. And tonight, as we have done before, America and our allies accept that responsibility.

Good night, and may God continue to bless America.

"There is no doubt that the United States can overthrow Saddam, but that does not mean we should."

An American Attack on Iraq Is Not Justified

John E. Farley

The following viewpoint was written in 2002 when Congress was considering a resolution (passed in October 2002) that would give President George W. Bush authority to use American military force against Iraq, both to enforce United Nations mandates calling for Iraq to destroy its weapons of mass destruction and to protect the United States from the "continuing threat" posed by Iraq's regime. In the viewpoint John E. Farley argues that American military action against Iraq cannot be justified on either moral or practical grounds. He contends that an attack on Iraq cannot be justified as a war of self-defense because Iraq has not attacked the United States or any of its allies. Farley also claims that such a war will not make America more secure and will likely exacerbate the geopolitical situation in the Middle East. The United States ultimately went to war against Iraq on March 19, 2003. Farley is a professor of sociology at Southern Illinois University at Edwardsville; he participated in protests against war in Iraq.

As you read, consider the following questions:

1. What historical moral principles would an attack on Iraq violate, according to Farley?
2. According to Farley, what national security risks would an attack on Iraq create?

True patriots do not follow their leaders blindly; rather they speak out when they see proposed actions by their leaders that threaten our country's best interests. President [George W.] Bush's request for a Congressional blank check for the United States to unilaterally attack Iraq is such an action.[1] An attack by the United States against Iraq would be bad for our country from a *moral/ethical* standpoint, from a *geopolitical* standpoint, from a *national security* standpoint, and from a *military* standpoint.

Morally and ethically, an attack against Iraq would be wrong, because it is not acceptable in a civilized world for one country to attack another when neither it nor its allies have been attacked. What is being proposed here is to attack Iraq because of what it *might* do, and this is wrong. Such an action would violate the historical principle that the United States does not attack other countries unless it, or one of its allies, is attacked. It would violate the international principle that all countries have a right to secure borders, and it would violate the tenets for just war laid out by most major world religions. The United States has long held that negotiation, not unilateral military action, is the means to resolve international disputes. To attack Iraq would be to turn our backs on this long-held view and to become a force for international violence, not international peace.

A Bad Precedent

In addition, an attack against Iraq would set a terrible international precedent: a precedent that if a country merely *feels* threatened by another country, it is OK to attack that country. Imagine the consequences if other countries follow this precedent. India and Pakistan feel threatened by one another, and have nearly gone to war. Were either to do what the United States proposes to do to Iraq, a nuclear war would be the likely result. And do we now want to tell the Russians, in effect, that [it] is OK to invade Chechnya because they feel threatened by it? Or to tell Egypt and Israel that it is now all right to launch "peremptory" attacks against

---

1. Congress passed a resolution in October 2002 giving authority to President George W. Bush to attack Iraq.

one another? A world in which countries attack one another merely because they feel threatened is a far more violent and dangerous world—not a world I want to live in!

Finally from a moral/ethical standpoint, it is important to point out that an attack on Iraq is something very different from U.S. action against the Taliban and Al Qaeda.[2] In the latter instance, we were attacked and were rightly acting to defend ourselves and bring the attackers to justice. Iraq is a completely different situation—in the case of an attack against Iraq, we become the attacker, and in so doing, surrender the moral high ground.

Negative Consequences

Geopolitically, an attack against Iraq makes no sense and would have serious negative consequences. For one thing, our allies in Europe and the Middle East and major countries around the world oppose such an action. France, Russia, Germany, China, and virtually all Arab and/or Muslim countries friendly to the United States have forcefully voiced their opposition to a U.S. attack on Iraq. These countries have supported us and helped us in the war on terrorism. We will lose much-needed support from around the world if we attack, and we will make potential enemies out of friends.

In addition, there are great perils in terms of the consequences in the Middle East of an attack on Iraq. It will provide cannon fodder for the most radical elements in Islamic societies, potentially destabilizing friendly governments in countries like Egypt and Saudi Arabia. In addition, an attack on Iraq would generally inflame passions in the Middle East, thus making the already-bad situation there, with repeated suicide bombings and violent Israeli retaliations, even worse. This is especially true if a U.S. attack on Iraq were followed by an Iraqi attack on Israel, as happened during the [1991] Persian Gulf War. This time, Israel says it will retaliate to any such attack. If this happens, it could cause a region-wide

2. Afghanistan's Taliban regime had provided a base of operations for Al Qaeda, an Islamic terrorist group responsible for the September 11, 2001, terrorist attacks. In late 2001 the United States attacked Afghanistan, helped install a new regime, and captured many Al Qaeda members.

war, and it will certainly fan the flames of resentment against the United States and Israel in the Middle East.

National Security Risks

An attack on Iraq also would make no sense from a *national security* standpoint. First and foremost, such an attack would detract from our efforts to dismantle Al Qaeda and bring [its leader] Osama Bin Laden to justice. Our success in this effort has been limited even without fighting two wars at once—Bin Laden and most of his highest lieutenants, unfortunately, remain at large. And from the standpoint of national security, we have already, tragically, seen that Al Qaeda and Bin Laden are by far the greater threat to the United States. They have taken over 3000 lives on U.S. soil; [Iraqi leader] Saddam Hussein has taken none.

Iraq Is Not an Imminent Threat

Unilateral military action by the United States against Iraq is unjustified, unwarranted, and illegal. The Administration has failed to make the case that Iraq poses an imminent threat to the United States. There is no credible evidence linking Iraq to 9/11. There is no credible evidence linking Iraq to Al Qaeda. Nor is there any credible evidence that Iraq possesses deliverable weapons of mass destruction, or that it intends to deliver them against the United States. . . .

The question is not whether or not America has the military power to destroy [Iraqi leader] Saddam Hussein and Iraq. The question is whether we destroy something essential in this nation by asserting that America has the right to do so anytime it pleases.

Dennis Kucinich, *Progressive*, November 2002.

While much of President Bush's argument for attacking Iraq is that Saddam might use weapons of mass destruction (WMD) against the United States, there is in fact no indication Saddam will use WMD offensively. In fact, the deterrence principle, used for 3 decades to keep the Soviet Union in check during the Cold War, ensures that he most likely will not. He wants to stay in power—and using WMD against the United States would mean a sure end to his power.

Additionally, an attack on Iraq carries real national security risks. If we attack Iraq, we will create an atmosphere that helps terrorists attract new recruits. Thus, an attack on Iraq could create many more Bin Ladens, who could present a threat of terrorism to the United States for decades to come.

Military Costs

Finally, an attack against Iraq makes no sense from a *military* standpoint. While Saddam is unlikely to use WMD offensively, he certainly could use them defensively, particularly if the point is reached where he figures he has nothing to lose. If WMD are used against U.S. troops invading Iraq, as they may well be, the casualties could be massive. In addition, it is likely that to overturn Saddam, urban warfare will be necessary. The casualties, both to U.S. troops and to Iraqi civilians, would be far greater in this type of warfare than is the case in most warfare. Tens of thousands of U.S. troops and hundreds of thousands of Iraqi citizens could die. Finally, there is the question of what would happen once we overturn Saddam. The Bush administration has expressed concerns about peacekeeping missions because of the high risk and long-term commitment that such missions entail. Yet an invasion of Iraq would necessitate a peacekeeping mission on a scale beyond anything the U.S. has undertaken thus far—a commitment that could last for decades. And without such a commitment, we could simply replace one Saddam with another.

There is no doubt that the United States *can* overthrow Saddam, but that does not mean we *should*. Indeed, from a moral/ethical standpoint, from a geopolitical standpoint, from a national security standpoint, and from a military standpoint, the costs far outweigh the benefits. I urge Congress to reject any authorization that allows the President to commit the United States to military action in Iraq without the support and cooperation of the international community through the United Nations Security Council. The costs of a unilateral U.S. attack on Iraq are simply too great.

"Americans understand that death and brutality will end only if American and British forces are successful."

Liberating Iraq's People from a Cruel Regime Justifies War

George W. Vradenburg

In the following viewpoint, written during the 2003 Iraq war, George W. Vradenburg argues that although war can be cruel and brutal, it can bring about beneficial change. He contends that a successful military action by American and British troops against the regime of Saddam Hussein will greatly improve the lives of Iraq's people by liberating them from a cruel and powerful dictator. Opponents of the war against Iraq, he maintains, fail to appreciate that war may be the only way to end the threat Hussein poses to his own people. Vradenburg is copublisher of *Tikkun*, a liberal Jewish magazine.

As you read, consider the following questions:
1. What examples does Vradenburg give in arguing against the "moral equivalency" between Iraq and the United States?
2. How does the author respond to the argument that war causes death and brutality?
3. What response does Vradenburg make to the argument that Hussein is not an immediate threat to the United States?

As Gabriel Garcia Marquez' famous book, *Love in the Time of Cholera*, revealed, extraordinary insights about love can emerge in the most horrible of circumstances. Seeing the brutality and killing of [the 2003] war on a daily basis naturally leads all of us to pray for a quick end to the pain and for a just peace. But the knowledge that the Iraqi people have been subjected to this brutality for over twenty years of [Saddam] Hussein's rule, and that America's success in the war holds out the hope for a better world for them, is reinforcing the American people's commitment to the path on which this country is embarked as well as their prayers for the rapid success of American and British forces.

Some in the antiwar movement condemn the brutality of the United States, implying that American success will prove no better a result for the Iraqi people than the rule of Saddam Hussein.

On that, I differ. And I differ with passion.

No More Equivalency

How can one compare a nation that embeds *reporters* within its troops to report its own conduct, with a nation that embeds disguised *para-military forces* within its civilian populations to take advantage of its adversary's humanity?

How can one compare a nation that provides emergency medical care *equally* to itself and its enemy, with a nation that executes enemy troops with a shot to the back of the head?

How can one compare a nation that uses its technology and skill to avoid civilian casualties, with a nation that shoots its own people in the back when they seek safety?

How can one compare a nation that risks the life of its young to save the natural resources and environment of another people, with a nation that seeks to destroy its country's natural resources and despoil its country's environment out of pique and anger?

There is no moral equivalency between two such nations.

Hussein's Brutality

There is no question that the daily fog of war is providing confusing snippets of information and pictures that are being experienced differently by peoples around the world. Indeed, some in the antiwar movement seem to explain the high levels of current support for President [George W.] Bush by accusing a "cheerleading" American press for misleading the American people about the brutality of war.

Right Triumphed over Wrong

Whether you were for or against this war, whether you preferred that the war be done with the [United Nations'] approval or without it, you have to feel good that right has triumphed over wrong. America did the right thing here. It toppled one of the most evil regimes on the face of the earth, and I don't think we know even a fraction of how deep that evil went. Fair-minded people have to acknowledge that.

Thomas L. Friedman, *New York Times*, April 27, 2003.

Americans aren't being misled. No one is confused. No one is ignoring the pain and suffering of fighters and civilians alike as a result of this war.

But Americans understand that death and brutality will end only if American and British forces are successful. If they are not, Hussein will, once again, visit death and brutality on his own people, and potentially on other peoples. Of this history leaves no doubt. Absent removal of Hussein, death and brutality will inevitably continue.

We cannot ignore the common humanity of mankind and our increasing interconnectedness by simply ignoring what Saddam Hussein has been doing to his people and his neighbors for over twenty years. The Iraqi regime claims that over 3,000 civilians have been injured by American bombing. But they killed over 50,000 civilians in Basra alone in 1991 after an uprising of Shia Muslims. And what of the hundreds of thousands of Kurds killed in 1988 from Hussein's use of chemical and biological weapons?

The only path to ending the suffering of the Iraqi people is the replacement of the Hussein regime with a government responsive to the welfare of average Iraqi citizens.

Are we truly committed to creating the environment and consciousness for a more loving and caring world, to "heal" a world in pain? If so, and if Saddam's removal will ease the pain of the Iraqi people, how can we bring that more caring environment about in Iraq without the use of force?

Some would argue that Hussein is not an immediate threat to the American people. But is there any doubt that he is an immediate threat to his own people?

Some would argue that UN [United Nations] inspectors should have been given more time to disarm Hussein of any weapons of mass destruction. But would that have disarmed Hussein of his capacity to continue a brutal and cruel repression of the Iraqi people?

Some would argue that the use of force to remove Hussein will create massive anti-American sentiment in the Arab world. But should we ignore the suffering of the Iraqi people because the steps needed to address that suffering run contrary to current popularity polls?

Protecting the Weak

Freedom is the best environment for a more loving and caring world. And freedom has never come without sacrifice and, yes the use of force. Freedom is dependent on the soldier willing to risk his life for peace.

A loving and caring world is dependent on the soldier who protects the innocent and the weak from the tyrant.

"A U.S.-led intervention, while liberating the Iraqi people, might well make everyone else less safe."

Liberating Iraq's People Does Not Justify War

Michael Massing

Michael Massing is a contributing editor for the *Columbia Journalism Review* and author of *The Fix*, a study of U.S. drug policy. In the following viewpoint, written before the 2003 war that deposed Saddam Hussein, he critically examines the argument that war would help Iraq's people by liberating them from an oppressive regime. In evaluating the justness of a U.S.-led invasion of Iraq, analysts must take into account not only anticipated benefits but also likely costs, he argues. Such costs include creating a new population of terrorists and enshrining the dangerous doctrine of preemptive war. Massing also questions whether the United States will expend the necessary resources *after* the war to properly rebuild Iraq. He concludes that nonviolent alternatives to war must be considered, even if they do relatively little to relieve the suffering of Iraq's people.

As you read, consider the following questions:

1. What moral quandary do liberals and leftists find themselves in concerning Iraq, according to Massing?
2. What distractions might a war on Iraq create, according to the author?
3. What aspect of the history of U.S. foreign relations with Iraq does Massing find troubling?

Michael Massing, "The Moral Quandary," *The Nation*, vol. 276, January 6, 2003, p. 17.

In late November [2002], the journalism department at New York University [NYU] hosted a forum on Iraq. The first five speakers, who included such liberal luminaries as historian Frances FitzGerald, cultural critic Todd Gitlin, former UN [United Nations] official Brian Urquhart and political scientist Michael Walzer, all expressed varying degrees of skepticism about the wisdom of invading Iraq. Then it was Kanan Makiya's turn. The son of a prominent Iraqi architect who came to this country in the late 1960s to attend MIT and never left, Makiya has spent the past fifteen years publicizing the horrors taking place in his native land. In *Republic of Fear* (1989) and *Cruelty and Silence* (1993) he chronicled the instruments of repression used by Saddam Hussein to brutalize his people and to suppress the Kurdish and Shiite uprisings after the Gulf War.

Now Makiya warned the audience of 200 that he would be striking a "discordant note" with the rest of the panel. "When you look at this coming war from the point of view of the people who are going to pay the greatest price—the people of Iraq—they overwhelmingly want it," Makiya declared. He discussed the steps he and other Iraqi exiles were taking to convince the Bush Administration to make the installation of a democratic government in Baghdad one of its chief war aims. And he urged those in attendance to support that goal. A war to overthrow Saddam, he said, "could have enormous transformative power throughout the Middle East." If there is even a "sliver of a chance—even 5 to 10 percent—that what I'm talking about might happen," Makiya said, those committed to bringing democracy and justice to the world have a "moral obligation" to support military action in Iraq. Amid applause from the audience, the other panelists shifted uncomfortably.

A Quandary for Liberals

Their discomfort is shared by many American liberals. For, on Iraq, the left finds itself in a quandary, torn between two fundamental principles. One is anti-imperialism—a deep suspicion of US military action abroad, especially when undertaken unilaterally. The other is humanitarianism—an impulse to see America use its influence to promote freedom and human rights around the world. In some cases, like Vietnam, the left has united under the anti-imperial banner; in others, like Bosnia, it has largely embraced the humanitarian standard. In Iraq, both principles seem to apply. How to weigh them? Only by coolly assessing the validity of the humanitarian and anti-intervention arguments can liberals hope to develop a position that is both coherent and defensible.

The humanitarian argument has been put forward most vigorously by Christopher Hitchens, which is unfortunate, since he's been unable to separate the issue from his own messy breakup with the left. . . .

But others have made the case for regime change more persuasively. One is [novelist] Salman Rushdie. No friend of US foreign policy, Rushdie, in an op-ed piece in the [Washington] Post, came out unequivocally for military action in Iraq. The case against Saddam, he wrote, is based on his decades-long "assault on the Iraqi people. He has impoverished them, murdered them, gassed and tortured them, sent them off to die by the tens of thousands in futile wars, repressed them, gagged them, bludgeoned them and then murdered them some more. Saddam Hussein and his ruthless gang of cronies from his home village of Tikrit are homicidal criminals, and their Iraq is a living hell." Rushdie added that "all the Iraqi democratic voices that still exist, all the leaders and potential leaders who still survive, are asking, even pleading for the proposed regime change."

Probably the strongest brief for intervention is *The Threatening Storm: The Case for Invading Iraq*, by Kenneth Pollack. A longtime analyst at the CIA who served on President [Bill] Clinton's National Security Council, Pollack favors intervention mainly for strategic reasons, viewing Saddam as so serious a threat to international peace and security that he must be removed. But Pollack's horror at Saddam's brutality pervades and shapes his argument. In his book, he grimly describes the techniques used by the Baathist regime to intimidate and terrorize the Iraqi people. Iraq, Pollack writes, has a dozen intelligence and security agencies employing up to 500,000 people. Torture, killing, rape, genocide and other cruelties are parceled out to as many of the regime's personnel as possible so as to implicate them in its crimes. Tortures include gouging out the eyes of children to force confessions from their parents, cutting out the tongues of critics to silence them and dragging in a man's wife or daughter to be raped in front of him. While ordinary Iraqis must subsist on their monthly ration cards, Saddam has, since the end of the Gulf War, built fifty new palaces with "gold-plated faucets and artificial rivers, lakes, and waterfalls that employ pumping equipment that could have been used to address the country's desperate water and sanitation problems." When Saddam's efforts to obtain a nuclear weapon are added in, Pollack writes, it's clear that both the Iraqi people and the world at large would benefit from his ouster. . . .

It's sometimes said that Saddam is just one of many tyrants around the world. Both North Korea and Saudi Arabia, our great ally, have equally odious regimes. Why single out Saddam? Well, Saddam clearly qualifies as a butcher, and the impossibility of unseating all the world's dictators seems an unconvincing reason not to seize the chance to depose one of them. When viewed from the perspective of a Kanan Makiya, the case for regime change in Iraq does indeed seem strong.

Weighing Costs and Benefits

But what about when that case is viewed from the standpoint of the rest of the world? In evaluating the justness of any military venture, it's critical to weigh the anticipated benefits against the expected costs. In the case of invading Iraq, those costs seem extremely high. A US-led intervention, while liberating the Iraqi people, might well make everyone else less safe.

To begin, there's the continuing threat from Al Qaeda [the terrorist group responsible for the September 11, 2001, attacks]. The mounting series of attacks on "soft" targets from Tunisia to Bali to Mombasa show how lethal the danger from militant Islam remains. Even so staunch an advocate of war as Kenneth Pollack believes that the United States should not confront Saddam until it has contained Al Qaeda. "Even if Iraq is only a few years from acquiring a nuclear weapon," he writes in *The Threatening Storm*, "the fact is that al-Qa'eda is attacking us right now and has demonstrated a capability that Saddam never has—the ability to reach into the US homeland and kill three thousand American civilians." Immediately after September 11, he adds, "we rightly devoted all of the United States' diplomatic, intelligence, and military attention to eradicating the threat from al-Qa'eda, and as long as that remains the case we should not indulge in a distraction as great as toppling Saddam.". . .

The Bush Administration's preoccupation with Iraq is similarly distracting it from the ongoing violence in the Middle East. War advocates maintain that ousting a tyrant like Saddam should not be held hostage to the fighting between Israel and the Palestinians, but only the most blinkered observer could fail to see how Washington's neglect of that issue is inflaming anti-American sentiment in the Arab world. . . . Writing in the *Financial Times*, Douglas Hurd, the former British foreign secretary, noted that a quick Anglo-American military victory in Iraq would result in "a sullen and humiliated Arab nation" that could lead to acts of violence against Israel and Western interests. Calling on the West to change its priorities, Hurd urged that the coming weeks be used "to galvanize the peace process and separate the terrorists from the majority of Arabs who still want peace. While the opportunity is still there we need to show that we in the west are concerned with justice for Palestine and security for Israel."

A US assault on Iraq could further incite Muslim extremists. Columnists like Jim Hoagland and Charles Krauthammer like to mock those who invoke the Arab "street." And it's true that most predictions of popular uprisings in the Arab world have proved wrong. But the main worry here is not a grassroots rebellion but a swelling of the terrorists' ranks. An American push toward Baghdad would provide an excellent recruiting tool for Al Qaeda. . . .

The Question of Rebuilding Iraq

Once the fighting stops, of course, the United States would face the monumental task of rebuilding Iraq. To do it right, Pollack maintains, America would have to station up to 100,000 troops in the country for five to ten years, at a cost of up to $20 billion, and spend another $5 billion to $10 billion in aid. Is the Bush Administration willing to make such a commitment? . . .

"If we're going to invade, the President has a responsibility to make his case—to explain how long it will take, and what resources we'll have to put in," says Mark Danner, who has written extensively about Haiti and Bosnia. "He's not doing that. We have to read about postwar plans in the *New York Times*. It's remarkable." Danner, who . . . joined such other liberals as Derek Bok, Aryeh Neier and Arthur Schlesinger Jr. in signing an ad in the *Times* opposing the war, says, "The most forceful argument for going to war is helping the Iraqi people. But that's not the reason for this war. I don't remember anybody in the Administration talking about the Iraqi people before August [2002]. Rather, it's about America's larger strategic goals in the region. They're going to get rid of this guy, then get out. During the 2000 campaign, George [W.] Bush was totally against nation-building. And I don't see any sign of change in that."

Britt. © 2003 by Copley News Service. Reprinted with permission.

Indeed, Kanan Makiya's vision for a post-Saddam Iraq seems excessively rosy. In his talk at NYU, Makiya noted that the democratic forces within the opposition Iraqi National Congress have received the most support from the more hawkish members of the Bush Administration: [vice president Dick] Cheney, [Secretary of Defense Donald] Rumsfeld and [deputy defense secretary Paul] Wolfowitz. This drew skepticism from fellow panelist Mansour Farhang. A former Iranian diplomat and staunch opponent of the current regime in Teheran, Farhang said the people of both Iraq and Iran would rejoice at seeing a new, democratic government in Baghdad. But, he quickly added, he doubted that America would actually install one. The Iraqi opposition, working in exile, "has had a thirty-year opportunity to create cohesive democratic organizations, and it has not done so. And now they're learning about democracy from Rumsfeld and Cheney?"

The history of US policy toward Iraq reinforces such doubts. Samantha Power, in researching her book "*A Problem From Hell*": *America and the Age of Genocide*, spent three years studying documents about the Anfal, Saddam's murderous campaign against the Kurds. Saddam's rule has been so abusive, she says, that Iraq has "sacrificed its right to sovereignty. If any of us lived in a country like that, we'd be praying for global rescue. We'd be looking up in the sky and hoping to see planes."

In the course of researching the Anfal, however, Power also saw declassified documents about the US response—or lack of it. At the time, Washington was tacitly backing Saddam in his war with Iran, and it did not want to endanger its ties to him. As one secret State Department report stated, "Human rights and chemical weapons use aside, in many respects our political and economic interests run parallel with those of Iraq." Some of the people responsible for making Iraq policy back then are in the current Administration, Power notes, and that makes her question the sincerity of their intentions toward the Iraqi people.

Moreover, Saddam, despite his brutal record, is not now carrying out the type of mass slaughter he did against the Kurds in the late 1980s. Iraq today is not like Rwanda in 1994, when Hutus were massacring Tutsis, nor Bosnia in the early and mid-1990s, when Serbs were killing Muslims. So, however cruel Saddam's regime might be, it is not perpetrating the type of atrocities that could normally justify a humanitarian intervention. For this reason, Human Rights Watch has not called for intervention in Iraq, as it did in the cases of Rwanda and Bosnia. . . .

Finally, there's the fundamental fact that we have not been attacked by Iraq—a major distinction with Afghanistan and Al Qaeda. If Saddam did obtain a nuclear weapon, of course, it would represent a major peril, but most experts agree that the threat is not imminent, undermining the Administration's case for a pre-emptive strike. "Pre-emption and imminence go together," Michael Walzer observed at the NYU forum. "Nobody expects an Iraqi attack right away, so there is nothing to pre-empt." Nor, he said, could a war against Iraq be considered just, according to the strict criteria for making such a judgment. . . .

Nonviolent Alternatives

There must be another way. One nonviolent alternative, proposed . . . by Andrew Mack (a former aide to UN Secretary General Kofi Annan), would seek to bolster the internal Iraqi opposition by lifting most of the sanctions on Iraq and opening up the country to foreign investment and other forms of international engagement. . . . A more hardheaded policy of "containment-plus," proposed by Morton Halperin and others, would combine an expansion of the no-fly zones in Iraq to cover the entire country, more intensive surveillance and inspections, and the use of precision airstrikes against targets not destroyed voluntarily on the ground. If evidence of an Iraqi nuclear program did emerge, a raid like the one Israel carried out in 1981 [against a suspected nuclear weapon facility]—this time with UN backing—could effectively dispose of it.

The great drawback of such an approach, of course, is that it would do little to relieve the suffering of the Iraqi people. Sadly, one might simply have to live with that. In the end, the moral case for intervening in Iraq is very strong, but not strong enough.

| *"This was liberation by deceit and misrepresentation."*

A Failure to Find Iraq's Weapons Calls into Question the Justification for War

David Corn

A central justification given by President George W. Bush and British prime minister Tony Blair for invading Iraq in 2003 was to find and destroy whatever weapons of mass destruction (WMD) that Iraq may have possessed. Bush and his backers accused Iraq of developing such weapons in violation of United Nations resolutions and argued that Iraq's WMDs posed an urgent threat to American and world security. However, no such weapons were found in the immediate weeks after the fall of Baghdad in April 2003. In the following viewpoint, published in May 2003, David Corn criticizes the lack of effort on the part of the American military to find weapons and secure nuclear facilities in Iraq. He asserts that the military's failure to make WMD search operations a priority raises questions about the Bush administration's real motives for going to war. Corn is the Washington editor for the liberal *Nation* magazine.

As you read, consider the following questions:
1. How have the statements of American officials on Iraq's weapons changed since before the 2003 war began, according to the author?
2. What question does Corn raise about the Bush administration?

David Corn, "Now They Tell Us," *The Nation*, vol. 276, May 19, 2003, p. 11.

My fellow Americans, there may be threatening amounts of weapons of mass destruction in Iraq. There may not be. We're not sure. And if they are there, it may take weeks after military victory before we can launch a major effort to find and secure them. By then, they could be gone—that is, if they were there in the first place—perhaps in the hands of people who mean us harm. And after we defeat Iraq's brutal regime, the people of Iraq will welcome US troops as liberators. Then again, within days, many of them could be shouting, "Yankee, go home" and calling for a new government dominated by fundamentalist religious leaders. We don't know. Nor do we really know the extent of any operational links between [Iraqi leader] Saddam Hussein and [the terrorist group] Al Qaeda—if such things exist. Still, I believe the potential risk posed by Saddam Hussein is so great that we cannot let what we do not know to stand in the way of decisive action. We cannot afford to guess wrong. With that in mind, I have ordered . . .

Clearing the Fog of Prewar

With Baghdad conquered, the fog of prewar has started to clear. And it now seems that had the Bush Administration been honest with the American public (and the world), its on-to-war pronouncements would have resembled the imaginary sequence above. Instead, [President George W.] Bush and his national security team—including ex officio members deployed in think tank bunkers and op-ed command centers—declared, without question or pause, that Iraq had dangerous levels of weapons of mass destruction and that it was "urgent," as Bush said, to find and destroy these weapons. They also talked about birthing a democratic government in Iraq without acknowledging obstacles and potential traps. But, it turns out, the Administration was not on the level. Moreover, it was woefully unready to deal with the consequences of military victory.

Though Bush and other war cheerleaders had spoken of liberating Iraq, their main argument concerned the threat posed by Saddam Hussein. The reason he was such an immediate danger, they said, was that he had these awful weapons and could, as Bush breathlessly noted, slip them to anti-American terrorists at any moment. Yet once US troops were in Iraq, the Bush Administration and the Pentagon adopted a rather lackadaisical approach to locating and securing such weapons. Weeks after the April 9 [2003] fall of Baghdad, the Pentagon was still in the process of assembling a survey team of 1,000 experts to search for chemical and biological weapons and signs of a nuclear weapons program. Why had this force not been ready to roll at the war's start?

During an April 17 press briefing, Defense Secretary Donald Rumsfeld said, "I don't think we'll discover anything, myself. I think what will happen is we'll discover people who will tell us where to go find it. It is not like a treasure hunt, where you just run around looking everywhere, hoping you find something. . . . The inspectors didn't find anything, and I doubt that we will." Imagine if Rumsfeld had said that before the war: We're invading another country to eliminate its weapons of mass destruction, but we won't find them unless people there tell us where they are.

Bush had maintained that Saddam Hussein was a danger partly because he was close to possessing nuclear weapons. The US military, though, did not bother to visit Iraq's number-one nuclear site. A *Washington Post* story noted that before the war the vast Tuwaitha Nuclear Research Center held about 4,000 pounds of partially enriched uranium and more than ninety-four tons of natural uranium, as well as radioactive cesium, cobalt and strontium. This is stuff that would be valuable to people seeking to enrich uranium into weapons-grade material or merely interested in constructing a dirty bomb. Yet, the paper reported, "Defense officials acknowledge that the US government has no idea whether any of Tuwaitha's potentially deadly contents have been stolen, because it has not dispatched investigations to appraise the site. What it does know, according to officials at the Pentagon and US Central Command, is that the sprawling campus, 11 miles south of Baghdad, lay unguarded for days and that looters made their way inside."

Most of the facilities suspected of being used to manufacture or store chemical and biological weapons have also gone unexamined. On April 28 British Prime Minister Tony Blair said, "We started off, I think, with around about almost 150 sites [to search] and we were beginning to look at seven of them. Actually, the sites that we have got as the result of information now is closer to 1,000. . . . We have looked at many of those, but nothing like a majority of them." Days earlier, Judith Miller, a *New York Times* reporter embedded with one of four specialized military teams looking for WMD, noted (low in the story) that "two of the four mobile teams originally assigned to search for unconventional weapons have since been reassigned to investigate war crimes or sites unrelated to weapons." Sure, war crimes are important. But more so than finding weapons that can kill thousands and that happened to be the basis for the invasion and occupation?

A Look of Urgency

Toward the end of April, Administration officials, speaking off the record, were telling journalists it was possible none of these terrible weapons will be found. Nothing had even been located at the sites the Secretary of State [Colin Powell] cited in his crucial briefing to the UN Security Council in February [2003]. Only about 150 actual WMD-seekers were then even at work within Iraq—and some were complaining they were short on vehicles, radios and encryption systems. Gen. Tommy Franks, commander of allied forces in the Persian Gulf, said the search process would take months and probably involve "several thousand sites."

At any moment, US forces may find convincing evidence of chemical or biological weapons—which undoubtedly will stir rousing cheers of we-told-you-so from war backers. But that won't be enough. War was waged—so Bush and others said—to prevent Iraq's WMD from being transferred to people and groups who would use them against Americans. But the war plan included no schemes to prevent that from occurring. This was a dereliction of duty. Looters beat the United States to Iraq's nuclear facility. If Iraq had WMD, if Al Qaeda types were in Baghdad, and if these terrorists were seeking weapons of mass destruction in Iraq—the fundamental claims made by the Administration—then there is a good chance the nightmare scenario Bush & Co. exploited to win support for their war has already come true.

Why is Richard Perlé not screaming about this from the roof of his French vacation house? Blair, for one, practically sounds bored with the topic of WMD. "Our first priority," he recently said, "has got to be to stabilize the country, the second is the humanitarian situation, and the third—and we can take our time about this and so we should—is to make sure that we investigate the weapons of mass destruction." Take our time? Wasn't the point that the United States and Britain could not wait one week longer before invading because it was necessary to neutralize the threat from these weapons?

Did President Bush Lie?

In justifying their war against Iraq, the Bush administration and its supporters based their case primarily on the threat to the United States posed by Iraq's weapons of mass destruction and ties with al-Qaeda. But to date [June 2003], American and British troops have found no signs of a chemical-, biological- or, more importantly, a nuclear-weapons program and have uncovered only low-level ties to al-Qaeda. And even if they subsequently find a few canisters of mustard gas, . . . it would hardly confirm America's claims that Saddam Hussein's regime posed a threat to the United States. On the contrary, the absence of weapons of mass destruction (WMD), in particular nuclear weapons, combined with the ease with which the United States rolled over the Iraqi army, strengthens the claims of administration critics that Hussein's regime could have been contained without going to war.

It also looks increasingly implausible that the Bush administration simply made an error of judgment in pressing its case against Iraq. Prior to the war, the United States failed to produce compelling evidence of Iraqi WMD or ties to al-Qaeda. According to United Nations weapons inspector Hans Blix, the evidence that the United States gave him of Iraq's WMD was "pretty pathetic." The Pentagon was also prepared for a short and easy war. That suggests that by the time of the invasion, the Bush administration was primarily concerned with advancing a geopolitical strategy in the region rather than defending Americans against future attack. In all likelihood, George W. Bush lied to the public about the dangers posed by Iraq.

John B. Judis, *American Prospect*, June 1, 2003.

So now they tell us. The Pentagon was not ready to go with an extensive WMD search-and-secure mission, and, after the war, there is no need to rush. And by the way, there might not be *any* WMD to show for all the effort.

Other Unpredicted Developments

The Administration was also unprepared—and disingenu-
ous—regarding another purported aim of the war: bringing
democracy to Iraq. In many cities, postwar dancing in the
street quickly turned to stomping in the street, as Muslim
clerics moved to gather political strength. But the rise of Shiite Power was not part of Bush's Iraq plan. Again, the *Washington Post*: "As Iraqi Shiite demands for a dominant role in
Iraq's future mount, Bush administration officials say they
underestimated the Shiites' organizational strength and are
unprepared to prevent the rise of an anti-American, Islamic
fundamentalist government in the country." But this was
hardly an unforeseeable event. "Nobody who knows anything about Shiites and Iraq are surprised by this," says Judith
Kipper, director of the Middle East Forum. "There were
people in the government who knew this. But they were on
the desks, not in the room where decisions were made.". . .

Such knotty matters were not covered by Bush and his
aides in their prewar speeches, which raised the rosy
prospect of a domino effect spreading democracy from post-
war Iraq to other states in the region. Nor did they address
the difficulties of providing security to postwar Iraq. In fact,
when Gen. Eric Shinseki, the Army Chief of Staff, testified
in February that this could require 100,000 or more troops,
Deputy Defense Secretary Paul Wolfowitz dismissed him as
being "wildly off the mark.". . .

Another now-they-tell-us jolt has been the cost of the war.
Before the invasion, Administration officials were fiercely
tight-lipped, refusing even to hazard a guess in public (as if
they couldn't even begin to estimate). In past weeks, the cost
projections have ranged as high as $20 billion a year for a to-
be-determined number of years. Despite Bush's prewar
pledge of "a sustained commitment" to Iraq, some US officials talk of a sooner-rather-than-later pullout. Of course,
that may conflict with the Administration's desire to have a
friendly government in Baghdad. Occupations can be confusing. But weren't we informed of that? Actually, no.

Loose chemical and biological weapons. Nuclear material
up for grabs. When-we-have-time WMD inspections. Those
restive Shiites. Twenty billion bucks a year. None of this made

it into Bush's prewar disclosure statement. War backers can—
and will—argue that the outcome was worth the costs and
the chaos. Indeed, the murderous Hussein is out; the Iraqi
people are fortunately no longer at his mercy. Yet this was
liberation by deceit and misrepresentation, and the scent of
fraud hangs in the air. It's a swindle that, for the time being,
benefited Iraqis but that undermined debate and democracy
at home. And with projecting American power still a priority for Bush and his crew, a question lingers: What else are
they not telling us?

6

"*The coalition's military action was the most rational response to Saddam Hussein's . . . policy of strategic deception.*"

War Was Justified Even If No Weapons of Mass Destruction Are Found

Michael Schrage

Iraq's development of weapons of mass destruction (WMD) was cited as a primary justification for the 2003 decision by the United States and Britain to end that country's regime by war. However, contrary to expectations, no evidence of such weapons were found during the war or in the weeks following its conclusion. In the following viewpoint analyst Michael Schrage argues that even if weapons of mass destruction are never found, war against Iraq was still justified. He contends that Saddam Hussein had engaged in a policy of strategic deception designed to create global uncertainty over whether or not he possessed WMD programs. Because other nations could never be sure just how dangerous Iraq was, Hussein was able to bully its neighbors and the world. By going to war, America announced that such brinkmanship would not be tolerated. Schrage is a senior adviser to the Security Studies Program at the Massachusetts Institute of Technology.

As you read, consider the following questions:

1. Why was Iraq's WMD threat credible for so long, according to Schrage?
2. Why was WMD ambiguity important for the survival of Hussein's regime, according to the author?

Russian President Vladimir Putin openly mocks America's failed efforts to find chemical, biological or nuclear weapons in Iraq. The Euroleft proclaims the coalition's rationale for invading the country—the presence of weapons of mass destruction (WMD)—a fraud. Top Iraqi scientists still swear that their country has no such weapons. No nukes, no anthrax, no VX gas. Are they liars trying to cut a better deal for themselves? Or might they simply be telling the truth?

It doesn't matter. If Iraq has significant WMD capabilities, they eventually will be discovered. But even if Iraq proves utterly free of WMD—or if it merely possesses a paltry two or three bio-weapons vans—the coalition's military action was the most rational response to Saddam Hussein's long-term policy of strategic deception. Hussein bet that he could get away with playing a "does he or doesn't he?" shell game with a skeptical superpower. He bet wrong.

The real story here is less about the failure of intelligence, inspections or diplomacy than about the end of America's tolerance for state-sponsored ambiguities explicitly designed to threaten American lives.

Does an American policy to deny unfriendly nation-states the policy option of creating ambiguity around WMD possession and the support of terrorism make the world a safer place? The Bush administration has made a game-theory-like calculation that it does. That's a calculation that could prove as important and enduring to global security as the Cold War's deterrence doctrine of "mutually assured destruction."

Iraq provides the single most important and dramatic case study in the Bush administration's efforts after [the terrorist attacks of] Sept. 11, 2001, to eradicate ambiguity as a viable strategic deterrent for unfriendly regimes. Hussein's Iraq may or may not have had impressive caches of nuclear, biological and chemical weapons. But his regime surely behaved as if it might. Iraq's WMD threat remained credible for more than 20 years because that's precisely what Hussein wanted the world to believe. After all, he had successfully deployed chemical weapons against both Kurds and Iranians. He'd earned his credibility.

Creating Uncertainty

Since his first gulf war defeat [in 1991], Hussein deliberately created uncertainty regarding the true nature of his regime's weapons programs. Iraq would alternately cheat and retreat and then concede and mislead. At great cost, it defiantly chose sanctions over inspections. To guarantee that the perennially volatile region remained on edge, Hussein regularly threatened to engulf his enemies in a "sea of fire." No one knew what he was really trying to do. That was precisely his point.

Even after [the terrorist attacks of] Sept. 11, the Afghanistan campaign[1] and the controversial "axis of evil" address,[2] Iraq took no public actions to reduce the level of ambiguity surrounding its WMD programs. To the contrary, it fought every U.N. initiative for inspections before reluctantly and churlishly acquiescing. Practically every demonstration of purported compliance seemed balanced by a calibrated act of defiance. When . . . Iraqi Gen. Hossam Mohammed Amin, who coordinated with the U.N. inspectors, declared in a January [2003] news conference that Iraq had destroyed various chemical weapons years ago, he simultaneously disclosed that Iraq had also destroyed all the records associated with destroying these weapons. This may even have been true. But it did nothing substantive to remove any WMD ambiguity. That Amin appeared to smile as he discussed the missing records didn't help.

This behavior by Iraq's regime was completely rational. Hussein's calculated cultivation of WMD ambiguity is a tactic torn directly from the tough-minded Cold War game-theory scenarios of nuclear deterrence. Brilliantly crafted by defense analysts such as former Harvard economist Thomas Schelling and the Rand Corp.'s Herman Kahn, this literature stresses the strategic importance of "signaling"—that is, the critical behaviors potential combatants choose to display to either clarify or obscure their ultimate intentions. For

1. In late 2001 America attacked Afghanistan and toppled its Taliban regime; that government had provided a base of operations for al-Qaeda, the terrorist group responsible for the September 11, 2001, terrorist attacks.   2. In his January 30, 2002, State of the Union Address, President George W. Bush singled out Iraq, Iran, and North Korea as part of an "axis of evil" for developing weapons of mass destruction.

years, "strategic ambiguity" worked very well for Hussein. His WMD ambiguity enhanced his survivability.

In fact, WMD ambiguity was at the core of Iraq's strategy. Why? Because if it ever became unambiguously clear that Iraq had major initiatives underway in nuclear or bio-weapons, America, Israel and even Europe might intervene militarily. If, however, it ever became obvious that Iraq lacked the unconventional weaponry essential to inspiring fear and inflicting horrific damage, then the Kurds, Iranians and Saudis might lack appropriate respect for Hussein's imperial ambitions. Ambiguity thus kept the West at bay while keeping Hussein's neighbors and his people in line. A little rumor of anthrax or VX goes a long way.

Why Inspections Could Never Work

Inspections agreements—no matter how coercive—never could have worked because they never addressed the fundamental issue: Hussein's desire to preserve WMD ambiguity in order to preserve Iraq's perceived influence and power.

Removing that ambiguity would have removed Hussein's ability to bully, bluster and blackmail the world. Perversely, U.N. Resolution 1441's poorly implemented inspection protocols fed the worst fears of both sides. Iraq's perfunctory compliance and deceitful history guaranteed that the United States would distrust the U.N.'s lackluster assurances of compliance. By contrast, Iraq's desire to be feared guaranteed that it would always manufacture just enough ambiguity to preserve its aura of menace. The inspectors' tortured attempts to appear evenhanded succeeded only in generating even greater ambiguities about both Iraq's willingness to comply and the weapons in its possession. And Secretary of State Colin L. Powell's dramatic yet desperate presentation before the U.N. Security Council was harshly attacked by critics who maintained that, yes, America's WMD evidence was inconclusively ambiguous.

Similarly, inspection proposals calling for "thousands" of intrusive inspectors, declaring all of Iraq a "no-fly" zone, and immediately bombing any sites that Iraq refused or delayed access to—acts of war in everything but name—seemed designed to ferret out WMD deceptions without in any way undermining the sovereignty or the totalitarian rule of the deliberate deceivers. Talk about a truly perverse outcome!

To the very end of his brutal regime, Saddam Hussein behaved as if preserving WMD ambiguity and preserving his power were one and the same. Even when he was directly threatened by the United States, his policy of WMD ambiguity remained unchanged. If he did have active WMD programs, he could at any time have quietly invited in French, Russian and German technicians to help dispose of them. Word would have gotten around. Or, after Sept. 11, he could have preemptively invited in U.N. inspectors as a prelude to lifting sanctions. Could he have done this without appearing weak? Yes. He could easily have preserved internal credibility by killing a few thousand more Kurds or chopping the ears off suspected dissidents. And regional balance-of-power issues could have been handled by a particularly brutal political assassination in Kuwait, for instance.

If Iraq really didn't have any WMD, Hussein's challenge would have been even easier. Several top Iraqi scientists could have left or "defected" to the West and talked about how their standard of living collapsed after Hussein stopped building weapons. Hussein could have allowed his French friends and Russian suppliers relatively free access to all parts of the country to further signal that he had nothing to hide. Of course, none of this happened. To the contrary, France unwittingly revealed just how effective Hussein's strategic ambiguity program was when its U.S. ambassador announced shortly after the war began that his country would support the coalition if the Iraqi leader used any weapons of mass destruction.

A Bluff?

But suppose Hussein was bluffing, suppose Iraq had no weapons of mass destruction of any significance. That shouldn't matter at all. To the contrary, why should the international community respect totalitarian brinkmanship based on a bluff? A brutal despot who bets his regime on a bluff deserves to lose everything.

America's diplomatic failure to reduce strategic ambiguity inevitably led to a military success that did. Those nation-states and regimes invested in bluff and "double games" to manage their relationships with the United States would be wise to learn from Iraq's experience that "preemptive ambiguity removal" is probably their optimal strategy for self-preservation. Syria's Bashar Assad may understand this in a way that North Korea's Kim Jong Il does not.

The Bush administration, appropriately interpreting Iraq's refusal to remove WMD ambiguity in violation of numerous international agreements as an overtly hostile act, has sent an unambiguous signal that it will take all steps necessary to eliminate such ambiguity. To be sure, this sort of policy may not inherently make the world a safer place. But policies that permit rogue states to wield greater influence by creating greater uncertainty about their weapons of mass destruction are guaranteed to make the world an even more dangerous place. Making every effort to increase the risks and reduce the rewards for regimes dependent on WMD ambiguity for their legitimacy should be a global responsibility—not just an American one.

"The invasion, occupation, and reconstruction of Iraq carries the United States across a fateful threshold."

The War on Iraq Heralded a Positive New Direction for American Foreign Policy

Thomas Donnelly

Thomas Donnelly is a resident fellow at the American Enterprise Institute and the editor of the institute's *National Security Outlook* newsletter. In the following viewpoint, written shortly after the conclusion of major combat operations in the 2003 war on Iraq, he analyzes the arguments for war made by President George W. Bush, concluding that the war marked a positive turning point in American foreign policy. He considers the war a prime example of the "Bush Doctrine"—the idea that repressive governments that threaten the United States should not merely be "contained" but changed, if necessary by military force. Donnelly defends Bush's decision to attack Iraq without explicit approval from the United Nations and argues that America should continue to use its military might to promote the expansion of freedom in the world.

As you read, consider the following questions:

1. What important elements of the Bush Doctrine were spelled out in the National Security Strategy document released in 2002, according to Donnelly?
2. What criticisms does the author make about the United Nations?

Thomas Donnelly, "The Meaning of Operation Iraqi Freedom," *National Security Outlook*, June 1, 2003. Copyright © 2003 by the American Enterprise Institute for Public Policy Research. Reproduced by permission.

We should remember how agonizing the post–Cold War period was in its uncertainty. Between the fall of the Berlin Wall in 1989 and the fall of Saddam [Hussein's] statues in 2003, a pall of ambiguity and indecision hung over the international political order. Yes, the United States was the world's sole remaining superpower, blessed with unprecedented wealth, military power, and a set of political principles based upon universal, individual political rights. It also had a uniquely intoxicating mix of "soft power"—spanning from the low culture of popular music to the high culture of the world's best research universities, and including seemingly everything in between as well. Yet translating this "hyperpower," as the French called it, into policies with a consistent purpose was not something American political leaders could easily manage nor something that American public opinion seemed to care that much about.

Until [the terrorist attacks of] September 11, 2001.

But though the terrorist attacks on the World Trade Center and the Pentagon galvanized Americans and the Bush administration to action, the scope of that action—beyond the first-order goal of bringing the terrorists themselves "to justice," as President [George W.] Bush put it—was still to be defined, and indeed it is still a work in progress.

The invasion, occupation, and reconstruction of Iraq carries the United States across a fateful threshold, one that we cannot easily go back across without suffering a tremendous defeat. The decision to step into Iraq reflects the character of President Bush himself—this is surely a case where an individual makes a great difference to history—as well as that of his advisers and, very profoundly, the nature of America, its power, and its principles. As we look for "lessons learned" from the war in Iraq and predictions as to what the immediate future might hold, it is best to begin with a careful reading of recent history.

The Road to War

The Bush Doctrine came to full flower in September 2002 with the release of the National Security Strategy [NSS], which originates in the observation that "the United States possesses unprecedented—and unequalled—strength and influence in the world." The Bush administration intended to keep it that way, to extend "the unipolar moment" as far as possible: "We will work to translate this moment of influence into decades of peace, prosperity, and liberty."

One purpose for the continued exercise of American global power, the NSS stated, is to defend against the world's new threats. But the strategy statement also foresaw an opportunity to exercise "a distinctly American internationalism"—a phrase first used in November 1999 by then-Governor George W. Bush in a speech at the Reagan Library. Most remarkably, the NSS argued that this "American internationalism" reflects "the union of our values and our national interests. The aim of this strategy is to help make the world not just safer but better." In other words, the Bush administration's drive to extend the Pax Americana can be found in a nexus of moral *and* strategic imperatives.

As attention—particularly congressional attention—turned toward Iraq, pressure began to mount on the administration to speak directly about its intentions toward the regime of Saddam Hussein. The anniversary of the September 11 attacks provided the president with the opportunity the moment demanded, and he seized it in speeches on September 11, 2002, at Ellis Island and the next day in an address to the UN General Assembly. Taken together, these two speeches mark the beginning of the march to war.

Quite naturally but with a clear purpose, the president began his Ellis Island speech by summoning and shaping the memory of the previous year's attacks: "September 11, 2001 will always be a fixed point in the life of America," he said. "The loss of so many lives left us to examine our own. Each of us was reminded that we are here only for a time, and these counted days should be filled with things that last and matter." For Bush, the "mission and moment" that began in the aftermath of 9/11 had not ended in Afghanistan, but continued; indeed, he now defined it as a lifetime commitment and perhaps an eternal one for the United States. The life of the nation, he seemed to suggest, should be filled with great things.

This was also perhaps the point where the Bush Doctrine parted ways with the [President Bill] Clinton past. Both presidents were animated by the vision of a liberal international order in which the United States played a central role. But Bush called for something like Theodore Roosevelt's version of "the strenuous life," a conscious striving to achieve a larger and more secure liberal order; Clinton, with his emphasis on economic forces and international organizations, acted as though the Pax Americana would somehow expand itself, requiring only modest efforts—in particular, modest military efforts—wise guidance, and constant consultation with others, whether democratic or autocratic. Bush's rhetoric also revealed a faith in what Abraham Lincoln might have called "providence." Said the president: "I believe there is a reason that history has matched this nation with this time." He explained,

There is a line in our time, and in every time, between those who believe all men are created equal, and those who believe some men and women and children are expendable in the pursuit of power. There is a line in our time, and in every time, between the defenders of human liberty and those who seek to master the minds and souls of others. Our generation has heard history's call, and we will answer it. . . .

This nation has defeated tyrants and liberated death camps, raised this lamp of liberty to every captive land. We have no intention of ignoring or appeasing history's latest gang of fanatics trying to murder their way into power. They are discovering, as others before them, the resolve of a great country and a great democracy. In the ruins of two towers, under a flag unfurled at the Pentagon, at the funerals of the lost, we have made a sacred promise to ourselves and to the world: we will not relent until justice is done and our nation is secure. What our enemies have begun, we will finish.

The speech was more than a moving oration at a solemn moment. It introduced, forcefully, new elements into the policy debate over Iraq and the "war on terrorism." No longer was this simply measuring justice for the September 11 attacks or a strategic decision to respond to the threat of rogue regimes and weapons proliferation. The president strove to place this larger war within the broadest context of American history, quoting the Declaration of Independence, recalling World War II in his references to "death camps" and "appeasement," and evoking the resolve of Lincoln in the Gettysburg Address—another funeral oration intended not simply to commemorate the dead but to dedicate the nation to a future, unfinished task.

Speaking to the United Nations the next day, the president shifted his emphasis to the threat posed by Iraq. Global security, he declared, is "challenged by outlaw groups and regimes that accept no law of morality and have no limit to their violent ambitions." Saddam Hussein's Iraq was a perfect example of this new threat: "In one place—in one regime—we find all these dangers, in their most lethal and aggressive forms, exactly the kind of threat the United Nations was born to confront."

How the War Changed the Middle East

Certainly the geopolitical calculus in the Middle East has visibly improved, including for Israel. We have 100,000 soldiers positioned on the border with Iran—a country now surrounded by reform governments in Afghanistan and Iraq, and one whose restive population is itself reportedly eager for liberalization. Already the United States has turned renewed attention toward the Syrian occupation of Lebanon and the sanctuaries enjoyed by the terrorist cadres of Hamas and Hizbullah; Syria itself may soon be confronted with democracies to the north, south, and east. There are thus grounds for thinking that, combined with other initiatives, our efforts in Iraq might end by so changing realities in the Middle East as to bring about the emergence of more than one new consensual government in the region.

Victor Davis Hanson, *Commentary*, June 2003.

But as he reviewed the history of Iraqi actions since the 1990 invasion of Kuwait, the president expanded the "threat theme" to demonstrate that Saddam's intentions and arsenal were dangerous not only in themselves but also to the authority of the United Nations itself. "Iraq has answered a decade of UN demands with a decade of defiance," he said. "All the world now faces a test, and the United Nations a difficult and defining moment. Are Security Council resolutions to be honored and enforced, or cast aside without consequence? Will the United Nations serve the purpose of its founding, or will it be irrelevant?"

Bush went on to lay out six tests to measure whether Iraq

intended to come into compliance with UN resolutions. Yet the president also made it clear that the removal of Saddam's regime was an inevitable outcome. Either the Iraqis would accept UN resolutions—"the just demands of peace and security"—or "action will be unavoidable," and the United States would go to war. "The purposes of the United States," said President Bush, "should not be doubted." And even if the regime complied, the Iraqi people would rid themselves of the tyrant. Saddam could not survive, either way, for "a regime that has lost its legitimacy will also lose its power."

Importantly in an international forum, Bush began to make the larger case for political reform in the Islamic world. "If we meet our responsibilities, if we overcome this danger, we can arrive at a very different future," he said.

> The people of Iraq can shake off their captivity. They can one day join a democratic Afghanistan and a democratic Palestine, inspiring reforms throughout the Muslim world. These nations can show by their example that honest government, and respect for women, and the great Islamic tradition of learning can triumph in the Middle East and beyond. And we will show that the promise of the United Nations can be fulfilled in our time.

In the event, however, the United Nations collectively demonstrated it had no interest in fulfilling this promise. Indeed, the Bush administration's decision to seek UN support proved a setback to the policy of regime change in Iraq. Although enjoying initial success in winning a unanimous vote in the Security Council for Resolution 1441, which found Iraq in "material breach" of previous UN resolutions and promised "serious consequences" for Iraq if it did not quickly come into compliance, the diplomatic process became a referendum on weapons inspections. . . . The United Nations revealed that it inherently favored sovereignty over liberty; perhaps the very structure of the organization—it is, after all, a collection of states—made it unfit to accomplish the purposes the president intended. And as one report of inspectors followed another, and as France led an opposition movement both in the United Nations and in the larger court of world opinion, the main question became one of American "unilateralism." The accelerating deployment of U.S. military forces to the region seemed to underscore Bush's "rush to war."

Thus, by the 2003 State of the Union address, President Bush found himself very much on the defensive. To regain the initiative, he again argued that the Iraq crisis was a test of the United Nations and that his patience with diplomacy was limited: "America's purpose is more than to follow a process—it is to achieve a result," he said. "[T]he course of this nation does not depend on the decisions of others. Whatever action is required, whenever action is necessary, I will defend the freedom and security of the American people." He continued:

Almost three months ago, the United Nations Security Council gave Saddam Hussein his final chance to disarm. He has shown instead utter contempt for the United Nations, and for the opinion of the world. The 108 UN inspectors were not sent to conduct a scavenger hunt for hidden materials across a country the size of California. The job of inspectors is to verify that Iraq's regime is disarming. It is up to Iraq to show exactly where it is hiding its banned weapons, lay those weapons out for the world to see, and destroy them as directed. Nothing like this has happened.

He also stressed his commitment to a free Iraq. "Tonight I have a message for the brave and oppressed people of Iraq: your enemy is not surrounding your country—your enemy is ruling your country. The day [Saddam Hussein] and his regime are removed from power will be the day of your liberation." And, as before at crucial moments, the president upped the political ante. Addressing another "message" to the U.S. armed forces, he left little doubt that war was imminent:

Many of you are assembling in or near the Middle East and some crucial hours may lie ahead. In those hours, the success of our cause will depend on you. Your training has prepared you. Your honor will guide you. . . . Sending Americans into battle is the most profound decision a president can make. The technologies of war have changed; the risks and suffering of war have not. For the brave Americans who bear the risk, no victory is free from sorrow. This nation fights reluctantly, because we know the cost and we dread the days of mourning that always come.

With the die so obviously cast, the one issue left to discuss was the real purpose of the war. Trapped in a dead-end debate about weapons inspections, the administration sent Secretary of State Colin Powell before the UN Security Council to try to preserve any hope of a wartime coalition of traditional Western allies. His presentation on February 5 [2003] was a dramatic show of satellite photographs, intercepts of Iraqi military radio communications, and information provided by Iraqi defectors. Not only did Powell make the case that Iraq had not disarmed, he also suggested that Saddam's links to terrorist organizations were substantial and increasing. "My colleagues," Powell beseeched in conclusion, "we have an obligation to our citizens—we have an obligation to this body—to see that our resolutions are complied with." Iraq had been given a last chance and spurned it, Powell said. "We must not shrink from whatever is ahead of us. We must not fail in our duty and our responsibility for the citizens of the countries that are represented by this body."

Yet for all its drama, the effort was an immediate failure. The echoes of Powell's presentation had barely died within the UN building when other members of the Security Council voiced skepticism about the facts of the case and continued opposition to the policy. Powell "failed in front of the world to prove that [Saddam] is a threat to the world," declared Jacques Myard, a member of the French parliament. "The U.S. really lost a great opportunity today." For others, evidence of weapons was simply a reason for more intense inspections. Over the following weekend, at the Wehrkunde conference in Munich—traditionally an expression of NATO and particularly German-American solidarity—German Foreign Minister Joschka Fischer spat at U.S. Defense Secretary Donald Rumsfeld, "Excuse me, I'm not convinced!"

The Bush Doctrine in Iraq

With the disarmament debate lost beyond saving, despite the steadfastness of British prime minister Tony Blair and indeed most European governments outside France and Germany, the Bush administration braced itself and the American people for the inevitability of a "unilateral" war. True, Great Britain could be relied upon to provide genuine support, and Kuwait, Qatar, and other small Persian Gulf states would permit U.S. forces a minimum of access and support, but Operation Iraqi Freedom had become Bush's War. Having failed to convince the rest of the world of any imminent threat from Saddam Hussein's Iraq, the president chose to cut his losses—to turn his back on the traditional diplomatic approach of Powell—and stress those arguments that appealed to fundamental American political principles. It was, in the president's reckoning, the despotic nature of the Iraqi regime that was the source of the danger. President Bush's February 26 speech to the American Enterprise Institute is worth quoting at length:

> The safety of the American people depends upon ending this direct and growing threat. Acting against danger will also contribute greatly to the long-term safety and stability of our world. The current Iraqi regime has shown the power of tyranny to spread discord and violence in the Middle East. A liberated Iraq can show the power of freedom to transform that vital region, by bringing hope and progress into the lives of millions. America's interests in security and America's belief in liberty both lead in the same direction: to a free and peaceful Iraq. . . .
>
> There was a time when many said that the cultures of Japan and Germany were incapable of sustaining democratic values. Well, they were wrong. Some say the same of Iraq today. They are mistaken. The nation of Iraq—with its proud heritage, abundant resources and skilled and educated people— is fully capable of moving toward democracy and living in freedom.
>
> The world has an interest in spreading democratic values, because stable and free nations do not breed the ideologies of murder. They encourage the peaceful pursuit of a better life. And there are hopeful signs of a desire for freedom in the Middle East. Arab intellectuals have called on Arab governments to address the "freedom gap" so their peoples can fully share in the progress of our times. Leaders in the region speak of a new Arab character that champions internal reform, greater political participation, economic openness and free trade. And from Morocco to Bahrain and beyond, nations are taking genuine steps toward political reform. A new regime in Iraq would serve as a dramatic and inspiring example of freedom for other nations in the region.
>
> It is presumptuous and insulting to suggest that a whole region of the world—the one-fifth of humanity that is Muslim—is somehow untouched by the most basic aspirations of life. Human cultures can be vastly different. Yet the human heart desires the same good things, everywhere on Earth. In our desire to be safe from brutal and bullying oppression,

human beings are the same. In our desire to care for our children and give them a better life, we are the same. For these fundamental reasons, freedom and democracy will always and everywhere have greater appeal than the slogans of hatred and tactics of terror. . . .

Much is asked of America in this year 2003. The work ahead is demanding. It will be difficult to help freedom take hold in a country that has known three decades of dictatorship, secret police, internal divisions and war. It will be difficult to cultivate liberty and peace in the Middle East, after so many generations of strife. Yet, the security of our nation and the hope of millions depend on us, and Americans do not turn away from duties because they are hard. We have met great tests in other times and we will meet the tests of our time.

This is a speech that Bill Clinton, or indeed almost any American president, might have made; it is imbued with liberal political principles that the founders would recognize as essentially the same as their own. Yet, coming from Clinton's mouth, these words would elaborate what he would regard as very good reasons for avoiding a war. For George W. Bush, these were fighting words.

Operation Iraqi Freedom

And soon after the president spoke them, Operation Iraqi Freedom did indeed drive Saddam Hussein's regime from power—opening an opportunity for what is the harder task of remaking Iraqi society and politics. The combination of American power and principles forged under the Bush Doctrine has transformed U.S. strategy in Iraq and the greater Middle East; we are no longer content to "contain" petty tyrants or "absorb" terrorist attacks from radical Islamists such as Osama bin Laden. To use Cold War terminology, America's purpose is now to "roll back" these forces.

This larger project is now also the defining trend of international politics. The Bush administration insists, rightly, that each crisis—including confrontations with the remaining "axis of evil" states, Iran and North Korea—will demand a unique approach. The Bush Doctrine does not free the United States or its presidents, diplomats, and soldiers from the practice of practical statecraft. But if the means may change (and the military preeminence of the United States, now shown in the Iraq war to be still greater than almost anyone imagined, suggests that Bush's view of the utility of force will endure), the ends—regime change and the promotion of democracy and individual political liberty—may not.

The aftermath of the war is also making clear the lasting rationale for the operation: the liberation of Iraq. The search for weapons of mass destruction has proved frustrating, even bungled. The anticipated humanitarian crisis, mercifully, did not materialize. And the war-for-oil myth has perhaps suffered most: Iraq's oil infrastructure is in a miserable condition and will require many years and billions of dollars of investment to return to past levels of production; Western companies are, for the immediate moment, taking a wait-and-see approach until greater security, rule of law, and a stable and self-governing Iraq emerges. Conversely, the full dimensions of Ba'ath repression—the mass graves, torture chambers, "disappearances"—are stunning in scope and still make for daily headlines. The Shiite pilgrimage to Kerbala was a genuine expression of religious sentiment by millions and frustrated what were almost certainly Iranian-aided attempts to politicize the event as an expression of anti-Americanism. And the number of small political parties that survived the terror and are coming out of the Iraqi woodwork is a challenge to catalogue.

A New Cause

The Bush administration has raised the stakes with the war in Iraq—both for itself and its successors. Already, the Bush Doctrine has freed us from the ingrained balance-of-power thinking of the Cold War and post–Cold War eras. In its rejection of containment and deterrence, it has likewise restored to prominence the historic characteristics of American national security policy: a proactive defense and the aggressive expansion of freedom. In its explicit focus not only on tearing down Saddam Hussein's terror state, but on raising up the lives of the long-suffering Iraqi people, it has pledged the United States to an ambitious, far-reaching course. It is a course from which we cannot, and should not, turn back.

"*Even putting aside the serious moral and legal issues raised by the U.S. invasion of Iraq, America is probably less secure as a result.*"

The War on Iraq Heralded a Dangerous New Direction for American Foreign Policy

Stephen Zunes

Stephen Zunes is a professor of politics and chair of the Peace and Justice Studies program at the University of San Francisco. His books include *Tinderbox: U.S. Middle East Policy and the Roots of Terrorism*. In the following viewpoint he argues that President George W. Bush's 2003 decision to go to war with Iraq has not made America any safer, especially from terrorist groups, and has isolated the United States from the rest of the world. He argues that the United States should end its occupation of Iraq and should pursue a foreign policy based on human rights and international law rather than on unilateral military force.

As you read, consider the following questions:

1. Why is there a growing resentment among Iraqis against America's military presence in Iraq, according to Zunes?
2. How might the war on Iraq spur the growth of terrorist groups, in the author's view?
3. What foreign policy changes does Zunes recommend?

Stephen Zunes, "The U.S. and Post-War Iraq: An Analysis," *Foreign Policy in Focus*, May 2003. Copyright © 2003 by the Interhemispheric Resource Center and the Institute for Policy Studies. Reproduced by permission.

There has been a disturbing degree of triumphalism following the [April 2003] overthrow—perhaps "evaporation" is a better word—of Saddam Hussein's regime in the face of invading American forces. Even putting aside the appropriateness of this kind of gloating in the face of such death and destruction—including thousands of civilian casualties—it is striking that few people are asking whether the U.S. or the rest of the world is safer now as a result of this overwhelming American military victory.

Operation Iraqi Freedom has about as much to do with freedom as *Sports Illustrated*'s annual swimsuit issue has to do with marketing swimwear: it is little more than an afterthought, a rationalization, and a cover for the hegemonic designs of the Bush administration and its Republican and Democratic supporters in Congress.

Yet the other rationalizations simply did not have much credibility. The supposed threat to American and regional security from the much-talked-about Iraqi arsenal of weapons of mass destruction (WMD) appears to have been a ruse. No such weapons have been found thus far, likely validating the assessment of many independent strategic analysts, key Iraqi defectors, and former chief UNSCOM [United Nations Special Commission] weapons inspector Scott Ritter that Iraq's WMD program had been effectively dismantled.

Likewise, no significant Iraqi link to the al Qaeda network has been established. Even before the invasion, Bush administration claims of Iraqi backing for terrorist groups contradicted prior assessments by the State Department and various U.S. intelligence agencies. Now, despite the capture of many thousands of Iraqi documents and the interrogation of Iraqi intelligence officials, there appears to have been no significant Iraqi support for terrorist groups for more than a decade.

There was never any debate about the repressive nature of Saddam Hussein's regime and the genuine relief that many Iraqis feel regarding the end of the pervasive climate of fear that had gripped the country for a generation. At the same time, it is significant that Iraqi celebrations over the regime's collapse have been relatively muted. A few hundred celebrants in a city of five million should not be portrayed as representing the sentiments of the population as a whole. Indeed, outside of some Kurdish areas of Iraq, there has not been much gratitude expressed by the population in response to the U.S. invasion. Though some American analysts have drawn analogies to the fall of the Berlin Wall and the overthrow of the communist regimes of Eastern Europe, those 1989 celebrations were much larger and more enthusiastic. There is a big difference between tearing down the statues of an ousted dictator yourself and having it done by an invading army.

Distrust of the United States

Even putting aside the tens of thousands of Iraqis who have engaged in anti-American demonstrations in recent weeks[1]—some of which have been met by gunfire from U.S. occupation forces—there is a pervasive sense of ambiguity among ordinary Iraqis regarding the U.S. invasion and occupation. What few Americans are willing to recognize at this stage is the fact that most Iraqis—including strong opponents of Saddam Hussein's regime—simply do not trust the United States.

Such mistrust is not unfounded. Consider the following:

- Washington backed Saddam Hussein during the height of his repression in the 1980s, concealing Iraqi atrocities—such as the chemical weapons attack against Halabja and other Kurdish towns—and supporting Iraq in its invasion of Iran.
- The U.S. targeting during the 1991 Gulf War bombing campaign went well beyond what was necessary to force Iraqi occupation forces from Kuwait. It included the destruction of key sectors of Iraq's civilian infrastructure, such as irrigation systems, bridges, and water purification plants. There were also thousands of accidental noncombatant deaths from bombs and missiles that landed in civilian areas.
- The U.S.-led economic sanctions that followed the war made it difficult for Iraqis to obtain spare parts to repair the damage to their civilian infrastructure and to provide medicines and other necessities for the general popula-

1. in April and May of 2003

tion. Although Saddam Hussein certainly shares the blame for the humanitarian disaster that resulted—estimates of deaths from malnutrition and preventable diseases run well into the hundreds of thousands—most Iraqis believe that U.S. policy actually strengthened Saddam's grip on power and caused unnecessary suffering among ordinary Iraqis.

- The recent U.S. invasion resulted in additional thousands of civilian casualties, both from the initial air assaults as well as from actions by American occupation forces, who have shot into vehicles of unarmed civilians approaching roadblocks and have fired into crowds of demonstrators.
- U.S. occupation forces failed to live up to their obligations under the Fourth Geneva Convention to maintain order, to provide adequate health care and other basic services, and to protect antiquities in the face of chaos and looting. Nothing could be more emblematic of U.S. priorities, in the eyes of many Iraqis, than the way U.S. forces immediately secured oil fields and the Iraqi Oil Ministry yet stood by while looters snatched priceless artifacts from museums and cleaned out hospitals of crucial medicines and equipment.
- Washington has thus far refused to allow the United Nations to play a significant role in the political restructuring of Iraq, insisting that it be primarily a U.S. role to chart the country's future. This raises concerns among many Iraqis, rightly or wrongly, that the U.S. will reorganize their country pursuant to America's economic, strategic, and ideological interests without adequate input by the Iraqi people themselves.
- The historical failure of the U.S. to support democracy in the Arab world raises serious questions as to whether Washington is really interested in democracy in Iraq. The U.S. still maintains close military, diplomatic, and economic ties with repressive governments in Saudi Arabia, Egypt, Oman, and other Arab countries, and Washington is a major supporter of Israeli occupation forces in the Arab-populated West Bank and Gaza Strip.
- The tendency for American policymakers to view free-

dom as encompassing not just political liberties but also commercial "economic freedom" limits the ability of other nations to protect their domestic industries and natural resources from control by powerful foreign corporations. Already, American companies are being brought in for what the Bush administration refers to as "reconstruction," and they appear to be settling in to play a major ongoing role in the Iraqi economy for many years to come.

As a result of all these and other factors, there is clearly a growing degree of resentment toward the American military presence in Iraq. A significant number of Iraqis are still sympathetic with the principles of the long-ruling Baath Party, which is rooted in Arab nationalism, anti-imperialism, and socialism. Although Saddam Hussein was to Baathism what Josef Stalin was to Marxism—both came to power through advocacy of a populist and egalitarian ideology that was subverted by a brutal totalitarian governing apparatus and a cult of personality—the original ideals of the movement still have widespread appeal.

Filling a Power Vacuum

Perhaps more significantly, the power vacuum left by the collapse of Saddam's dictatorship has cleared the way for social and political organizations led by Shiite clerics, who—unbound by the more egalitarian structure in Sunni Islam—can take advantage of their hierarchical organizational structure to mobilize quasigovernmental institutions. Centered in the mosques, which even Saddam Hussein's dreaded secret police could not totally disrupt, these Shiite clerics—unlike most secular opposition leaders—were able to survive the repression. In many respects, the situation in Iraq today parallels that of Shiite-populated Iran following the collapse of the autocratic regime of the shah in 1978–79, when Shiite *komitehs* [morality police] were able to effectively build the infrastructure of a new government based along theocratic lines, even though the revolution itself was broadly based. Within slightly more than two years, hard-line Shiite leaders solidified their control over Iranian government and society, resulting in an extraordinary wave of repression that has been weakened only gradually in recent years.

Although leadership by Shiite clergy and their supporters does not necessarily mean that Iraq will follow the radical and repressive model of Iran, Shiite Muslims do constitute the majority of the country's population and firmly believe that their time has come to rule Iraq after centuries of Sunni domination. Ironically, there are indications that the U.S. is rehabilitating much of the Baath Party, including Saddam Hussein's police, as a counterweight to the growing Shiite clerical influence. Even though top leaders of the old regime are still wanted men, U.S. forces are beginning to see the remaining Baath Party apparatus as the only entity in the country with the organization and experience to pose a challenge to the emerging Shiite leadership.

Much of the Baath Party consists of individuals who joined solely for career advancement, to take advantage of various perks, or to try to save themselves and their family from persecution. But most members still believe in the party's nationalistic and anti-imperialist principles and will join with the Islamists in challenging American rule. Indeed, as the British learned early last century during their occupation of Iraq after displacing the Ottoman Turks, Iraqis harbor a deep resentment of occupying powers from the West.

A Safer World

There is a very real possibility, then, that a low-level armed insurgency could develop in the coming weeks and months, not from loyalists of Saddam Hussein's regime but from ordinary Iraqis demanding self-determination and an end to the U.S. occupation. For this reason, there may be no one happier that U.S. forces have invaded and occupied Iraq than [terrorist] Osama bin Laden, who now has Americans where he wants them: in the heart of the Arab-Islamic world and resented by hundreds of millions of people who see this invasion as an act of imperialism. Indeed, if there was any logic behind the madness of [the terrorist attacks of] September 11, 2001, it may have been the hope that the U.S. would be provoked to launch such an invasion and that it would spark a dramatic growth in anti-American sentiment throughout the region.

If this was indeed the plan, it appears to be working. The

U.S. has squandered the unprecedented sympathy of the international community in the immediate aftermath of 9/11 and faces the prospect of unprecedented hostility today. This shift alone should challenge the assumption that the invasion of Iraq has somehow made the U.S. safer.

Meanwhile, North Korea—once it found itself on the Bush administration's "axis of evil" list along with Iraq, which it saw was about to be overrun—has decided to break its commitment to halt its nuclear program, apparently in hopes of developing a credible nuclear deterrent to stave off a possible American invasion. Other countries may learn the same "lesson." As a result, the U.S. invasion of Iraq has probably increased rather than decreased the threat of nuclear proliferation.

The War's Primary Aim

The primary aim of the war, launched in defiance of the United Nations, was to demonstrate what is likely to happen to any leader, nation, community or people who persist in refusing to comply with US interests. Many propositions and memos about the vital need for such a demonstration were being discussed in corporate and operational planning circles well before Bush's fraudulent election, and before the terrorist attacks of September 11 [2001].

The term "US interests" can lead to confusion here. It does not refer to the direct interest of US citizens, whether poor or well-off, but to the far-reaching interests of the most powerful multinational corporations, often dominated by US capital, and now, when necessary, defended by the American military.

John Berger, *The Nation*, May 12, 2003.

Bush administration claims that the U.S. invasion of Iraq would somehow advance the possibility of Arab-Israeli peace appear to be without any foundation. Iraq has in recent years had virtually no role in relation to the decades-old conflict in the lands hundreds of miles to the west. [Palestinian leader] Yasir Arafat and the Fatah leadership have long resented Saddam Hussein's support during the 1980s and early 1990s of the Abu Nidal faction, which was responsible for the murder of a number of prominent Fatah leaders.

Regarding the widely publicized allegation that the Iraqi

government was paying money to the families of Palestinian terrorists who are killed, the amount of money Saddam Hussein offered these Palestinian families was far less than what they normally lose in the destruction of their houses by Israeli occupation forces, as is the normal fate of families of terrorists. Nor is Iraq the largest donor to these families; U.S. allies like Saudi Arabia contribute even more money. Finally, the bulk of the Iraqi money goes to families of Palestinian civilians and militiamen killed by Israeli occupation forces during clashes in the West Bank and Gaza Strip, not the families of terrorists. These financial donations were largely part of an effort to gain Iraqi sympathizers among this highly politicized population and encourage support for the tiny pro-Iraqi Palestinian faction known as the Arab Liberation Front. It probably had no impact on the number of suicide bombings and other acts of terrorism against Israelis. Like other opportunistic Arab dictators, Saddam Hussein has long given lip service to the Palestinian cause but has actually done little in practice.

The U.S. invasion of Iraq has merely highlighted Washington's hypocrisy in demanding that Iraq disarm its weapons of mass destruction and abide by UN Security Council resolutions while refusing to insist that Israel do the same.

Still, in proving that the U.S. can decisively defeat any Middle Eastern government that challenges American prerogatives, policymakers hope that—as a result of the Pentagon's overwhelming and devastating display of force—those who oppose U.S. hegemony will somehow now meekly accept American dictates. However, the more likely result will be an increased sense that the nation-state is incapable of resisting American hegemony, and it is therefore up to nonstate actors utilizing various forms of asymmetrical warfare—such as terrorism—to fight back. And, as has already become apparent in the ongoing and protracted war against al Qaeda, defeating a decentralized network of underground terrorist cells is a lot more difficult than defeating the Republican Guard.

An Alternative Security Agenda

In summary, even putting aside the serious moral and legal issues raised by the U.S. invasion of Iraq, America is probably less secure as a result. What, then, can the Bush administration do now to advance America's security interests?

- The U.S. should turn interim governance of the country over to a United Nations administration that will pave the way for Iraqi self-rule. There is precedence for just such a UN role in the two-year transition of East Timor from its devastating 24-year occupation by Indonesia to independence. . . . With the entire international community, including other Arab states, represented in the world body, UN efforts to build up a functioning civil society and representative political system would be more likely to succeed. The eventual Iraqi government would have far greater legitimacy in the eyes of both Iraqis and the international community if it developed under UN administration; otherwise, it would appear—rightly or wrongly—to be simply a puppet regime of the United States.

- The U.S. should support the establishment of a weapons of mass destruction–free zone throughout the Middle East. Such regionwide disarmament regimes have already been established in Latin America and the South Pacific. A WMD-free zone throughout the Middle East has been endorsed both by U.S. allies Egypt and Jordan and by the potentially hostile regimes of Iran and Syria.

- U.S. security operations in the Middle East should be restricted to the real threat: the al Qaeda network. This would primarily require improving intelligence and interdiction, with the use of force restricted to small targeted paramilitary operations where appropriate. Since such efforts would be greatly enhanced through the cooperation of Middle Eastern states, pursuing policies that are less inclined to alienate the governments and peoples of the region would seem logical.

- The U.S. needs to vigorously support a sustainable peace between Israelis and Palestinians, recognizing that security for Israel and rights for Palestinians are not mutually exclusive but are in fact mutually dependent. Although Washington should continue to insist that Palestinian violence—particularly acts directed toward Israeli civilians—cease unconditionally, the Bush administration must also insist that Israel live up to its international obligations by withdrawing from its illegal settlements in the occupied territories, giving up control of the West Bank and Gaza Strip in order to establish a viable Palestinian state, sharing Jerusalem as the co-capital of both countries, and negotiating a fair resolution to the plight of Palestinian refugees.

- The U.S. must support the establishment of democratic governments throughout the Middle East, which will require—among other things—suspending military and economic aid to all countries that engage in gross and systematic violations of internationally recognized human rights. Although Washington should not try to impose its form of democracy on other countries, a natural evolution toward greater political pluralism in the region will far more likely emerge if the U.S. ends its current support for autocratic governments and occupation armies. As President John F. Kennedy warned, "Those who make peaceful evolution impossible make violent revolution inevitable."

- To set right U.S. policy toward Iraq would not only put the United States more into line with international law and international public opinion, it would be in the national security interests of the country. There is also a more fundamental question as to who we are as a nation. Today's debate regarding the U.S. role in the world in many ways parallels one that took place just over a century ago when the U.S. invaded the Philippines. Leading intellectuals of the day, such as the writer Mark Twain, formed the Anti-Imperialist League, whose central question was, "What kind of a nation should we be: a republic or an empire?"

- The bottom line is this: The U.S. must pursue a foreign policy based more upon human rights, international law, and sustainable development and less on military conquest and occupation, arms transfers, and the profiteering of U.S.-based corporations. Developing such a new posture in the Middle East would not only be more consistent with America's stated values, it would also make us a lot safer.

Periodical Bibliography

The following articles have been selected to supplement the diverse views presented in this chapter.

Spencer Ackerman and John B. Judis	"The First Casualty: The Selling of the Iraq War," *New Republic*, June 30, 2003.
Mohammed Aldouri	"Iraq States Its Case," *New York Times*, October 17, 2002.
Phillip J. Brown	"Justice, Law, and War," *America*, August 18, 2003.
Juan Cole	"Questions of Peace and Genocide," *Tikkun*, May/June 2003.
Charles Colson	"Just War in Iraq: Sometimes Going to War Is the Charitable Thing to Do," *Christianity Today*, December 9, 2002.
Thomas R. Eddlem	"War Under False Pretense," *New American*, August 11, 2003.
Thomas L. Friedman	"The Meaning of a Skull," *New York Times*, April 27, 2003.
Reuel Marc Gerecht	"A Necessary War," *Weekly Standard*, October 21, 2002.
Bill Keller	"The Boys Who Cried Wolfowitz," *New York Times*, June 14, 2003.
Michael T. Klare	"It's the Oil, Stupid," *Nation*, May 12, 2003.
Dennis Kucinich	"The Bloodstained Path," *Progressive*, November 2002.
Jim Lacey	"Hide and Seek . . . and Seek: Where'd Those Weapons of Mass Destruction Get To?" *National Review*, June 16, 2003.
Michael Lerner	"The Triumph of Fear," *Tikkun*, March/April 2003.
Arno J. Mayer	"Beyond the Drumbeat: Iraq: Preventive War, 'Old Europe,'" *Monthly Review*, March 2003.
Johanna McGeary	"Dissecting the Case: The Administration's Rationale for War with Iraq Is Based on New and Old Evidence—as Well as Passionate Conviction," *Time*, February 10, 2003.
National Review	"At War: Closing the Case," September 16, 2002.

National Review	"Weapons of Mass Destruction: Deceptions About Deception," July 14, 2003.
Joseph S. Nye	"Before War," *Washington Post*, March 14, 2003.
Richard Perle	"The United States Must Strike at Saddam Hussein," *New York Times*, December 28, 2001.
Jonathan Schell	"The Case Against the War," *Nation*, March 3, 2003.
Arthur Schlesinger Jr.	"The Immorality of Preventive War," *Los Angeles Times*, August 26, 2002.
Andrew Sullivan	"So Where Are They?" *Sunday Times* (London), June 1, 2003.
Miroslav Volf	"Indefensible War," *Christian Century*, September 25, 2002.

CHAPTER 2

What Role Should the United States Play in Iraq?

Chapter Preface

In a November 2002 cover story in the *Atlantic Monthly* titled "The Fifty-first State," journalist James Fallows noted that a decision to go to war with Iraq with the purpose of destroying the regime of Saddam Hussein would mean that Iraq would "have claims on American resources and attention . . . comparable to those of any U.S. state." Predicting (correctly) that in the event of war the United States military would be victorious and that Hussein's government would be overthrown, Fallows argued that once the war was over, "Iraq would become America's problem, for practical and political reasons. . . . Conquered Iraqis would turn to the U.S. government for emergency relief, civil order, economic reconstruction, and protection of their borders."

President George W. Bush appeared to confirm Fallows' contention in a speech televised to the Iraqi people on April 10, 2003. Although he promised Iraqis that America had no intention of conquest and that "the government of Iraq . . . will soon belong to you," Bush stated that U.S. and allied forces would remain in Iraq to "help maintain law and order" and "to help you build a peaceful and representative government."

An obvious question facing both Iraqis and Americans was exactly how long U.S. troops and other personnel would need to be stationed in Iraq to achieve Bush's promises. One historical precedent was America's occupation of Japan following World War II. That occupation, in which General Douglas MacArthur served as the military governor of Japan, lasted seven years. The occupation, Fallows writes, was "a slow, thorough effort to change fundamental social and cultural values, in preparation for a sustainable democracy." Americans were intimately involved in writing Japan's constitution, rewriting Japanese labor laws, designing the education curriculum, and other tasks. Few Americans have envisioned or called for a similar seven-year effort in postwar Iraq. Whether a shorter and less intrusive occupation could achieve Bush's stated goal of a unified Iraq under a free and representative government remains an unanswered question. The viewpoints in this chapter highlight some of the debates over America's proper role in rebuilding Iraq after the 2003 war.

"*We may have had enough troops to win the war—but not nearly enough to win the peace.*"

The United States Is Failing to Establish Order in Iraq

Philip Carter

The following viewpoint was written shortly after the end of major hostilities in the 2003 U.S.-led war on Iraq. With Saddam Hussein's regime destroyed and its leaders either captured, killed, or missing, the United States faced the problem of maintaining order and stability in the nation. Philip Carter argues that while the United States had deployed enough troops to wage a successful war against Hussein's regime, it underestimated the number of soldiers necessary to prevent widespread lawlessness and chaos in Iraq once the war was over. Such problems should have been anticipated based on past U.S. peacekeeping experiences in Bosnia and Afghanistan, he contends. Carter, a law student and former army officer, writes frequently on legal and military issues.

As you read, consider the following questions:
1. What events in Iraq could have been prevented with more American soldiers, according to Carter?
2. What lessons does the author say should be derived from America's experiences in Bosnia, Kosovo, and Afghanistan?
3. What parallel does Carter draw between warfighting and manufacturing?

During the lead-up to the [2003] Iraq war, hawkish Pentagon appointees like Deputy Defense Secretary Paul Wolfowitz predicted that the conflict could be won with as few as 50,000 troops. Meanwhile, senior generals like Army Chief of Staff Eric Shinseki and CENTCOM Commander Tommy Franks said that it would take at least 200,000 for the offensive and far more to police and rebuild the country after victory. For a brief week at the end of March [2003], as U.S. troops met stiff resistance in Nasiriya and found their supply lines harassed in the south, it seemed the generals' doubts about fighting the war on the cheap might be confirmed in the worst way. Then, almost overnight, resistance collapsed. That rapid victory proved the contention that Defense Secretary Don Rumsfeld had been pressing for more than two years: that America's new high-tech, highly mobile military could win wars with far fewer troops and armor than traditional war-fighting doctrines called for—and with far fewer casualties. (At the height of the war, the United States and the United Kingdom had just 90,000 combat troops in the country.) That was a crucial test of the broader Bush administration policy of using America's military might to crush determined foes rather than simply "managing" them, as previous administrations were wont to do. If America could "preempt" future threats without overextending its military, as Iraq seemed to show, then the argument for the Bush Doctrine would be vastly strengthened.

But the hawks' gloating proved premature. The generals' argument had never been just about what forces it would take to decapitate [Iraqi leader Saddam Hussein's] regime. It was also about being ready for the long, grinding challenge after the shooting stopped. By that measure they have been proven dizzyingly correct. April and May [2003] brought daily news reports from Baghdad quoting U.S. military officers saying they lacked the manpower to do their jobs. As the doubters predicted, we may have had enough troops to win the war—but not nearly enough to win the peace.

Victory Leads to Crisis

When victory arrived, we lacked the troops on the ground to prevent Baghdad—and most of the rest of the country—

from collapsing into anarchy. We had tanks and Bradley fighting vehicles galore in the capital, but not nearly enough soldiers to guard such facilities as the key ministries, hospitals, and the National Museum. Ministries torched and looted during the first days are now unavailable to house the planned interim government. The plunder of hospitals set the stage for a still very possible humanitarian crisis. Looters who ransacked the National Museum stole many of the priceless historic artifacts that connected contemporary Iraq with its ancient roots, inflicting a mammoth public relations disaster upon the United States.

Things have not gotten much better over the following weeks [of April and May 2003]. Lawlessness and chaos continue to reign. Women are raped, law-abiding citizens have their property stolen, those who have anything left don't go to work so they can guard what they still have. The prize the United States sacrificed so much to gain—freeing Iraq from Saddam and clearing the way for its democratic rebirth—is being squandered on the ground as ordinary Iraqis come to equate the American presence with violent lawlessness and immorality, and grasping mullahs rush into the vacuum created by our lack of troops. Mass grave sites, with no troops to secure them, have been unearthed by Iraqis desperate to find remnants of relatives killed by Saddam Hussein's regime, but those same Iraqis, digging quickly and roughly, may have inadvertently destroyed valuable evidence of human rights violations and crippled the ability of prosecutors to bring war criminals to justice. Perhaps worst of all, the prime objective of the entire invasion—to secure and eliminate Saddam's weapons of mass destruction capacity—has been dealt a serious blow. Even Iraq's publicly known nuclear sites had been thoroughly looted before American inspectors arrived, because, once more, not enough troops had been available to secure them. Radioactive material, perhaps enough to make several "dirty bombs," has now disappeared into anonymous Iraqi homes, perhaps awaiting purchase by terrorists. Critical records detailing the history and scope of the WMD program have themselves been looted from suspected weapons sites because too few soldiers were available to guard those places. "There aren't enough troops in the whole Army," said Col. Tim Madere, the officer overseeing the WMD effort in Iraq, in a recent interview with *Newsweek*. Farce vied with disaster when the inspectors' own headquarters were looted for lack of adequate security. Triumph on the battlefield has yielded to tragedy in the streets.

Belatedly recognizing their horrendous miscalculation, the Bush administration last month [May 2003] replaced the retired general in charge of Iraq's reconstruction, Jay Garner, with former diplomat L. Paul Bremer, who immediately called for 15,000 more troops to keep order. Even if he gets that many, however, Bremer will still be woefully short of the manpower he'll need to turn Iraq from anarchy to stable democracy.

The architects of the war might be forgiven for misgauging the number of troops required had the war come a dozen years ago, when the United States had little experience in modern nation-building. But over the course of the 1990s America gained some hard understanding, at no small cost. From Port-au-Prince to Mogadishu, every recent engagement taught the lesson we're now learning again in Iraq: America's high-tech, highly mobile military can scatter enemies which many times outnumber them, in ways beyond the wildest dreams of commanders just a generation ago. But it's not so easy to win the peace.

A Muscular Peace

Consider the lessons of Bosnia, Kosovo, and Afghanistan. In Bosnia, America won its war with a combination of muscular diplomacy, air power, and covertly armed Bosnian-Muslim and Croat proxy armies on the ground. That mix of tools brought about the Dayton Accords in the fall of 1995. But when it came to making that treaty work, America had to send in its heaviest armor divisions, putting a Bradley fighting vehicle on nearly every street corner to enforce the peace. NATO [North Atlantic Treaty Organization] initially sent 60,000 soldiers into Bosnia, and almost eight years after Dayton, America still has several thousand soldiers on the ground in Bosnia, as part of a 13,000-soldier NATO force. Winning hearts and minds took a backseat to overawing malcontent factions with an overwhelming and, for all intents and purposes, enduring show of force.

Like Bosnia, Kosovo was taken without any American ground commitment. There the United States won its [1999] war by unifying air power with what now-retired Gen. Wesley Clark calls "coercive diplomacy." But to win the peace America had to send in substantial ground forces. NATO quickly deployed a force of nearly 50,000 troops to the tiny province that is roughly 1/40 the size of Iraq. Truly pacifying Kosovo—a process that has really only just begun—means leeching it of its toxic ethnic hatreds and endemic violence. Most indicators hint that NATO will have to maintain its mission in Kosovo for at least a generation.

The Risk of Chaos

Perhaps it's churlish to say this so soon after an impressive military victory, but America may have underestimated the risk of chaos in postwar Iraq. . . .

Experience in Albania, Tajikistan and the former Yugoslavia underscores the idea that when dictators fall, the pressure cooker can explode.

General Eric Shinseki, the U.S. Army chief of staff, infuriated the Pentagon's civilian leaders by saying that several hundred thousand troops might be needed to police postwar Iraq. But Shinseki knows this subject—he commanded peacekeeping forces in Bosnia—and he looks smarter each day.

"Now that Saddam is gone," mused Imad Saleh, 30, a businessman who is delighted by the dictator's departure, "everything has gone crazy."

Nicholas D. Kristof, *International Herald Tribune*, April 12, 2003.

In Afghanistan, the pattern was much the same. It took only 300 U.S. special forces on foot and horseback—supported by 21st-century aircraft, GPS-guided bombs, and a force of Northern Alliance fighters—to bring down the Taliban. But once the government in Kabul had fallen, thousands of U.S. and allied troops had to come in to secure the country. Today [in June 2003], 15,000 American and allied soldiers remain there, 50 times more than it took to win the war.

Even the failures of these previous missions demonstrate that manpower is less important to the achievement of military victory than to coping with victory's aftermath. In Kosovo, according to retired Gen. Montgomery Meigs, then commander of the Balkan stabilization force, we were forced to "do less" because the Pentagon claimed it could not send more peacekeeping troops. As a result, says Meigs, "we were unable to run operations inside Kosovo to interdict the internal movement of arms and Albanian-Kosovar fighters to [neighboring] Macedonia." Those armed separatists set off a civil war in Macedonia—stopped only by the timely deployment of more Western troops, including Americans, into that country.

Something very similar happened in Afghanistan.[1] Our biggest failure there occurred in the mop-up stage, following the flight of the Taliban government. Because we had so few troops on the ground, we failed to cut off and destroy the remnants of al Qaeda—including, most likely, [terrorist] Osama bin Laden himself—as they fled into the lawless mountain regions of the Afghan and Pakistani frontier. Our subsequent efforts at nation-building on the cheap have yielded similar results. Our unwillingness to put many troops on the ground has made a mockery of the president's promise for a "Marshall Plan" for Afghanistan. The Western-oriented, U.S.-installed president, Hamid Karzai, controls little more than [the capital city of] Kabul, and the rest of the country has already drifted back into warlordism.

Shooting the Inspectors

Not only did Wolfowitz and Shinseki publicly disagree over how many troops would be needed to win the war in Iraq, they also disagreed on how many troops would be needed to win the peace. Shinseki testified to Congress that we would need "several hundred thousand" and Wolfowitz, very publicly, argued that the situation called for far fewer. What's become clear in the aftermath is that Wolfowitz simply didn't grasp, as Shinseki (who's commanded Army units in peacekeeping operations) clearly did, just what this kind of

---

1. Following the September 11, 2001, terrorist attacks, which were carried out by operatives of the al Qaeda terrorist group, the United States attacked Afghanistan, where al Qaeda was based. The United States used air power and the support of Afghan insurgents to topple the country's Taliban regime.

mammoth peacekeeping and nation-building operation would entail.

First, the simple question of keeping order: "It's frustrating; we do not have the personnel or the training to be policemen," Army civil affairs Maj. Jack Nales told *The Washington Post* in Baghdad. In one encounter, Nales had to explain the lack of order to civilians. "I'm sorry the police agencies and judicial system isn't [sic] here. I'm sorry we don't have enough soldiers to help you."

Second, only a few soldiers—civil affairs specialists, military police, and medical and engineering units, mostly—are specially equipped for the actual work of nation-building. The vast majority of the rest provide security for these lightly armed units. An engineering platoon of 40 soldiers might need an entire company of infantry (120 men) for security, depending on the terrain. A lack of security entails cutting the number of nation-building missions. If only three infantry companies are available, then only three missions can be undertaken at any one time—essentially the problem in Iraq today.

Third, without a secure environment, no one else can do their job. Weapons investigators are hamstrung if they are constantly getting shot at or inspecting sites whose security evaporates the moment they leave. Oil crews and aid workers don't want to be shot on the job any more than soldiers do, and security concerns have slowed progress on every project in Iraq—from opening the port at Umm Qasr to reopening the oil fields at Kirkuk.

Young Men in the Mud

In many ways, the contrast between warfighting and nation-building resembles the difference between productivity in the manufacturing and service industries. Businessmen have long known that you can rather easily substitute capital and technology for labor in manufacturing. Until very recently, however, it's been far more difficult to do so for the service industries. A similar principle applies to military affairs. In war fighting, everything ultimately comes down to sending a projectile downrange. How you send the bullet (or bomb) makes a difference—you can use an infantryman with a rifle, or a B-52 launching a cruise missile. But the effect at the far end is the same—the delivery of kinetic or explosive energy. Over the last 50 years, American strategy has made increasing use of effective technology, substituting machines for men, both to reduce casualties and to outrange our enemies.

But this trading of capital for increased efficiency breaks down in the intensely human missions of peace enforcement and nation-building. American wealth can underwrite certain aspects of those missions: schools, roads, water purification plants, electric power. But it can't substitute machines or money in the human dimension—the need to place American soldiers (or police officers) on patrol to make the peace a reality.

On the shelf of nearly every Army officer, you'll find a book by retired Col. T.R. Fehrenbach on the Korean conflict titled *This Kind of War.* At the end of World War II, confronted by the military revolution brought on by the atomic bomb, America cut its military from a wartime high of 16 million down to a few hundred thousand. Bombs and airplanes—not soldiers—would now protect America's shores and cities. After fighting as a grunt in Korea, Fehrenbach thought otherwise. Transformation was great for the Air Force and Navy, but for the Army and Marine Corps, the essential nature of warfare remained unchanged.

"You may fly over a land forever; you may bomb it, atomize it, pulverize it and wipe it clean of life," wrote Fehrenbach. "But if you desire to defend it, protect it, and keep it for civilization, you must do this on the ground, the way the Roman legions did, by putting your young men into the mud." It's time Don Rumsfeld brushed up on his Fehrenbach. The book is on Gen. Shinseki's official reading list for the Army, so it's a good bet that one of his generals has a copy he can borrow.

*"The claims that progress is too slow . . .
[do] not reflect reality on the ground."*

The United States Is Successfully Establishing Order in Iraq

Vito Fossella

Vito Fossella is a New York Republican member of the U.S. House of Representatives. The following viewpoint was written after he visited Iraq a few weeks after Saddam Hussein was deposed in the 2003 war. Fossella argues that complaints that the United States was failing to "win the peace" in Iraq after its military triumph are unfounded and that everyday life was already improving for millions of Iraqis because of the presence of American soldiers and workers. He blames much of the hardship that Iraq's people are enduring not on the war or on American occupation, but on Hussein's regime, which he contends has neglected or destroyed much of Iraq's society and infrastructure. He asserts that the United States is committed to staying in Iraq for however long is necessary to establish a democracy—and is also committed to leaving Iraq once that task is complete.

As you read, consider the following questions:

1. What did the 2003 war on Iraq accomplish, according to Fossella?
2. What lesson does the author derive from America's experience with Japan and Germany after World War II?
3. What examples of improvements in the lives of Iraqis does Fossella describe?

It has been less than a month since the end of [2003] combat operations in Iraq and already the glass-half-empty crowd is portraying America as having won the war but losing the peace. I had the opportunity to visit Baghdad over the [2003] Memorial Day weekend with several of my House colleagues and witnessed American ingenuity and Iraqi determination firsthand.

The war eliminated a grave national security threat, deposed an evil dictator and liberated millions of people from oppression. Today [June 4, 2003], basic services throughout the country are being restored, a new democratic government is being planned and people no longer live in fear of punishment for expressing their thoughts or worshipping their religion. We applaud America's military and its allies for their courage and heroism in securing this victory.

The claims that progress is too slow, the situation unstable and the United States lacks the expertise to get the job done does not reflect reality on the ground in Baghdad, Kirkuk and beyond. Indeed, the critics who complain that the seeds of democracy will not take root in the sands of a desert where tyranny ruled are as wrong today as the pessimists were in 1945.

Changes Take Time

In the aftermath of World War II, Japan and Germany were nations utterly destroyed by war and with a long tradition of militaristic rule. With the unwavering support of the United States and its allies, Japan and Germany were reborn as full-functioning democracies within 10 years. Today, they stand as prime examples of freedom's power to lift up people economically and ensure tyranny's demise.

These changes did not occur overnight, and there were bumps in the road.

Likewise, Iraq will not be rebuilt in a matter of only four weeks, especially after the years of abuse Saddam Hussein inflicted on his people, their land and their natural resources.

Indeed, it is inaccurate to define the task before the United States as rebuilding alone when, in fact, much of our time will be devoted to building the basic infrastructure of the nation. During our visit, it was clear that many of the delays in restoring essential services were not the result of war, but rather neglect by the regime. So much of the country has been plundered by Saddam and his henchmen for their personal gain while many Iraqis live in abject poverty, unable to afford basic necessities such as food and medicine.

America's Promise to Iraq

America's promise to Iraq . . . is to be its partner, and to help Iraq move toward a representative government, one that respects the principles of justice, the rule of law and the rights of the Iraqi people. The U.S. will deliver on this promise, too, and will be with the Iraqis for as long as it takes—until the job is done. . . .

We also appreciate the many immediate difficulties that the Iraqis are facing, and are taking steps to mitigate the severity of their hardship. With freedom comes responsibility—including the responsibility of not taking the law into one's own hands, but dealing with grievances in an organized, lawful manner. To this end, we will work with Iraqis and others to achieve stability.

Zalmay Khalilzad, *Wall Street Journal*, April 17, 2003.

Under Saddam, 40 percent of the population did not have clean water to drink, more than 500,000 children were malnourished and 1 in 8 died before age 5. Half of Iraq's hospitals have disappeared in the past decade, 70 percent of its schools are in disrepair, and electricity in parts of the nation was as rare as the right to express one's mind freely.

Signs of Improvement

During our time in Baghdad and Kirkuk, it was clear everyday life already is improving for millions of Iraqis.

- Electricity: After living for decades with limited electric service, many Iraqis in the north and south have more power than before the war, and in Basra residents have power 24 hours a day. Electricity is also being supplied round-the-clock to public hospitals, water treatment plants and sewage facilities.
- Clean Water: In less than one month [after the end of major fighting of the 2003 war], Iraq's water system is running at 60 percent of prewar levels, and some parts of

the country report more water than ever before. Extensive repairs to water treatment facilities are under way and being supported by international aid organizations.

- Security: A secret police that tortured and killed at will has been replaced by approximately 5,000 officers who are patrolling Iraq's streets to maintain the rule of law rather than the rule of oppression. Eighteen police stations have been established and 25 more are expected to become operational shortly [as of June 2003]. In addition, the court system and prisons are functioning to maintain law and order.
- Health care: The people of Baghdad are receiving basic health care and no outbreaks of epidemics of cholera, dysentery and other diseases have occurred. Doctors and nurses have returned to work, warehouses full of medicine and supplies are available and a national vaccination program is being developed.
- Free elections: In the first steps toward self-government, 17 of 26 Interim Town Councils have been installed. The Iraqi people will increasingly assume greater control over their country's economic and political reconstruction as well as vast supplies of natural resources. Progress also is being made in forming a democratic national government that will protect religious freedom and represent Iraq's myriad ethnic groups.

The reconstruction of Iraq and the formation of a civil society that respects basic human rights must be measured in years, not weeks. Human liberty must be pursued over time, not clocked like a sprint. Even the American journey took time.

America's Commitment

The United States will fulfill its commitment to Iraq, and then we will depart, having liberated a nation, freed a people and established a democracy of the people, by the people and for the people.

"We'd better get used to U.S. troops being deployed there [in Iraq] for years, possibly decades, to come."

The United States Should Embrace an Imperialistic Role in Iraq

Max Boot

Max Boot is a foreign policy scholar and author of *The Savage Wars of Peace: Small Wars and the Rise of American Power.* In the following viewpoint he argues that the United States has the power and resources to rebuild Iraq after the 2003 war, provided that it is willing to expend them. The major obstacle to success, he contends, is America's reluctance to use its powers to impose order and democracy in Iraq for fear of being accused of imperialism. Boot defends American imperialism, arguing that the United States has a long and positive historical record of imperial control of foreign nations. A successful rebuilding of Iraq could require spending billions of dollars and the permanent stationing of American troops in that country, he concludes.

As you read, consider the following questions:
1. What response does Boot make to Secretary of Defense Donald Rumsfeld's comment on American imperialism?
2. How much money might be necessary to rebuild Iraq, according to the author?
3. What lessons does Boot say should be learned from America's experiences with nation-building in the 1990s?

What is the greatest danger facing America as it tries to rebuild Iraq: Shiite fundamentalism? Kurdish separatism? Sunni intransigence? Turkish, Syrian, Iranian or Saudi Arabian meddling?

All of those are real problems, but none is so severe that it can't readily be handled. More than 125,000 American troops occupy Mesopotamia [as of May 2003]. They are backed up by the resources of the world's richest economy. In a contest for control of Iraq, America can outspend and outmuscle any competing faction.

The greatest danger is that we won't use all of our power for fear of the "I" word—imperialism. When asked on April 28 [2003] on al-Jazeera whether the United States was "empire building," Secretary of Defense Donald Rumsfeld reacted as if he'd been asked whether he wears women's underwear. "We don't seek empires," he replied huffily. "We're not imperialistic. We never have been."

That's a fine answer for public consumption. The problem is that it isn't true. The United States has been an empire since at least 1803, when Thomas Jefferson purchased the Louisiana Territory. Throughout the 19th century, what Jefferson called the "empire of liberty" expanded across the continent. When U.S. power stretched from "sea to shining sea," the American empire moved abroad, acquiring colonies ranging from Puerto Rico and the Philippines to Hawaii and Alaska.

While the formal empire mostly disappeared after World War II, the United States set out on another bout of imperialism in Germany and Japan. Oh, sorry—that wasn't imperialism; it was "occupation." But when Americans are running foreign governments, it's a distinction without a difference. Likewise, recent "nation-building" experiments in Somalia, Haiti, Bosnia, Kosovo and Afghanistan are imperialism under another name.

A Force for Good

Mind you, this is not meant as a condemnation. The history of American imperialism is hardly one of unadorned good doing; there have been plenty of shameful episodes, such as the mistreatment of the Indians. But, on the whole, U.S. imperialism has been the greatest force for good in the world during the past century. It has defeated the monstrous evils of communism and Nazism and lesser evils such as the Taliban [in Afghanistan] and Serbian ethnic cleansing. Along the way, it has helped spread liberal institutions to countries as diverse as South Korea and Panama.

Yet, while generally successful as imperialists, Americans have been loath to confirm that's what they were doing. That's OK. Given the historical baggage that "imperialism" carries, there's no need for the U.S. government to embrace the term. But it should definitely embrace the practice.

That doesn't mean looting Iraq of its natural resources; nothing could be more destructive of our goal of building a stable government in Baghdad. It means imposing the rule of law, property rights, free speech and other guarantees, at gunpoint if need be. This will require selecting a new ruler who is committed to pluralism and then backing him or her to the hilt. Iran and other neighboring states won't hesitate to impose their despotic views on Iraq; we shouldn't hesitate to impose our democratic views.

Mixed Messages

The indications are mixed as to whether the United States is prepared to embrace its imperial role unapologetically. Rumsfeld has said that an Iranian-style theocracy "isn't going to happen," and President [George W.] Bush has pledged to keep U.S. troops in Iraq as long as necessary to "build a peaceful and representative government." After allowing a temporary power vacuum to develop, U.S. troops now are moving aggressively to put down challenges to their authority by, for example, arresting the self-declared "mayor" of Baghdad.[1]

That's all for the good. But there are also some worrisome signs. Bush asked for only $2.5 billion from Congress for rebuilding Iraq, even though a study from the Council on Foreign Relations and the James A. Baker III Institute for Public Policy estimates that $25 billion to $100 billion will be needed. Iraq's oil revenues and contributions from allies

1. Mohammed Mohsen al-Zubaidi, a former Iraqi exile who had proclaimed himself the mayor of the Iraqi capital without U.S. permission, was arrested by U.S. forces on April 27, 2003.

The Imperial Question

Iraq forces the imperial question. In the aftermath of an Iraqi war, it may suffice to install a friendly autocracy, withdraw the bulk of our forces, and exert our influence from afar. Yet some have called for more. . . . Many have argued that only a democratic transformation of Iraq, and eventually of the larger Arab world, can provide long-term security against terrorism and nuclear attack.

In an important address in February [2003], George W. Bush lent his voice to this chorus. In no uncertain terms, the president affirmed that "the world has a clear interest in the spread of democratic values," not least because "free nations do not breed the ideologies of murder." The president invoked the examples of American-led democratization in post–World War II Germany and Japan, and he pointedly rejected the claim that Arab nations are incapable of sustaining democracy. What the president did not say, yet gently and ambiguously implied, was that so deep a cultural change would require America to occupy Iraq in force and manage its affairs for years to come.

Stanley Kurtz, *Policy Review*, April 2003.

---

won't cover the entire shortfall. The president should be doing more to prepare the U.S. public and Congress for a costly commitment. Otherwise, Iraqis quickly could become disillusioned about the benefits of liberation.

The cost of our commitment will be measured not only in money but also in troops. While Bush and Rumsfeld have wisely eschewed any talk of an early "exit strategy," they still seem to think that U.S. forces won't need to stay more than two years. Rumsfeld even denied a report that the U.S. armed forces are planning to open permanent bases in Iraq. If they're not, they should be. That's the only way to ensure the security of a nascent democracy in such a rough neighborhood.

Does the administration really imagine that Iraq will have turned into Switzerland in two years' time? Allied rule lasted four years in Germany and seven years in Japan. American troops remain stationed in both places more than 50 years later. That's why these two countries have become paragons of liberal democracy. It is crazy to think that Iraq—which has less of a democratic tradition than either Germany or Japan had in 1945—could make the leap overnight.

The record of nation-building during the past decade [prior to 2003] is clear: The United States failed in Somalia and Haiti, where it pulled out troops prematurely. Bosnia, Kosovo and Afghanistan show more promise because U.S. troops remain stationed there. Afghanistan would be making even more progress if the United States and its allies had made a bigger commitment to secure the countryside, not just [the capital] Kabul.

If we want Iraq to avoid becoming a Somalia on steroids, we'd better get used to U.S. troops being deployed there for years, possibly decades, to come. If that raises hackles about American imperialism, so be it. We're going to be called an empire whatever we do. We might as well be a successful empire.

> *"The best way in which the U.S. and its allies . . . can make their historic contribution to the building of a new, . . . democratic Iraq is by helping remove our people's obsession with foreign intervention."*

The United States Should Reject an Imperialist Role in Iraq

Awad Nasir

Awad Nasir is an Iraqi poet. In the following viewpoint, written while a U.S.-led coalition was successfully waging a war in Iraq to topple the regime of Saddam Hussein in 2003, he argues that the United States and its allies should not impose military rule on Iraq for an extended period of time. America should instead work to effect a transition to an Iraqi-led government as soon as possible. Iraq's people, he contends, are capable of self-government and would create a government friendly to their American liberators.

As you read, consider the following questions:

1. How have Iraqi fears of foreign domination hampered the nation's development, according to Nasir?
2. What accounts for the swiftness of American victory in the 2003 war, according to the author?
3. How might a new democratic government in Iraq affect other Middle East countries, in Nasir's opinion?

As Iraq is liberated [from the rule of Saddam Hussein], the Iraqi people and the U.S.-led Coalition[1] face the task of creating a new government in Baghdad.

The short-term aim of such a government is to put the shattered nation together again. The longer-term aim should be genuine democratization, so no future tyrant can emerge.

Few people in the outside world, even among our Arab brethren, fully understand the depth of our sufferings at the hands of Saddam Hussein, known to Iraqis as "the Vampire" (al-Saffah). An Iraqi proverb says: He who is watching the club does not understand the one who is beaten with it.

Fear of Foreign Powers

Rightly or wrongly, most Iraqis believe that their sufferings are, at least in part, a direct result of the support given by foreign powers to the various despots who seized and exercised power in Baghdad. Fear of foreign intervention has been a central theme of Iraqi politics, literature, and art ever since the country came into being after the First World War.

That fear often paralyzed the Iraqi political parties and movements and provided an excuse for tyrants to push issues such as human rights, democratization, and pluralism out of the national discourse. The standard claim was that a nation that faced the threat of foreign domination could not afford the luxury of internal debate and dissent in the context of a democratic system.

Should we allow that claim to be revived and reinvigorated by insisting on direct American military rule in Baghdad?

Most Iraqis agree that the U.S.-led liberators cannot—indeed should not—just walk away as soon as "the Vampire" is killed or captured. The U.S. and its allies must play central roles in rebuilding the Iraqi economy and helping our people develop the institutions of democracy.

The best way in which the U.S. and its allies, notably Great Britain, can make their historic contribution to the building of a new, free, and democratic Iraq is by helping re-

1. The United States enlisted forty-five other nations to support the 2003 war in Iraq. Great Britain and Australia were the only ones to furnish a significant number of troops.

move our people's obsession with foreign intervention. That, of course, cannot be achieved through the imposition of an Anglo-American military rule beyond the minimum period that all reasonable people accept as necessary.

Problems with Prolonged U.S. Rule

Prolonged American military rule in Baghdad could . . . antagonize Iraq's neighbors, especially Turkey and Iran. Both can cause nuisance and endanger Iraq's territorial integrity and national sovereignty.

More importantly, there is no evidence that a majority of Iraqis will welcome American rule even for 18 months. An army of liberation could turn into an army of occupation almost instantly.

Amir Taheri, *National Review Online*, April 7, 2003.

Can Iraqis rule themselves?

There are some who say "No." They base their claim on pseudo-political mumbo-jumbo according to which the destruction of Iraqi civil society by Saddam Hussein has drained our nation of the resources it needs to create a people-based government.

Anyone with any intimate knowledge of Iraq would know that claim to be not true. Iraqi people have been fighting Saddam Hussein's tyranny since 1968, long before the U.S. and the rest of the world got wise to his evil schemes and methods.

The ease with which the U.S.-led Coalition captured virtually the whole of Iraq in two weeks is, at least in part, due to the fact that the overwhelming majority of our people did not, would not, fight in support of their oppressor.

Today, the U.S. and its allies have almost all of the 24 million Iraqis as their friends.

This is why whoever forms the future government of Iraq will be a friend of its liberators. Our people will not allow it to be otherwise.

A Short Period of Transition

The U.S. and Britain should start urgent talks with all Iraqi political parties and personalities to form an interim authority to work alongside the allies during a period of transition that should be as short as possible.

Iraq has the largest urban middle class in the Arab world. It has tens of thousands of qualified people, both inside and outside the country, to help create and run a new democratic system. All those could be mobilized in the service of a new Iraq with the help and guidance of the liberating forces.

The U.S. and Britain should remember that the liberation and democratization of Iraq could mark the start of a new phase in the history of the Middle East as a whole.

They have to confound Saddam's villainous apologists who have been shouting all along that the Anglo-Americans came to Iraq only for its oil. They must prove wrong the French and others who have been telling the Arabs that Washington has a hidden agenda to colonize Iraq.

An Iraqi government backed by the U.S., Britain, and their 40 other "willing" allies will be bad news for the region's despots and terrorists, and good news for its long-suffering nations.

A democratic and prosperous Iraq under a government of its choosing could become [the] only true friend of the United States in the Arab world. It could also inspire the people of other Arab countries, as well as neighboring Iran, to fight for their own freedom and in pursuit of their own democratic aspirations.

"We must internationalize our policies for rebuilding a postwar Iraq."

America Must Involve the United Nations in Rebuilding Iraq

Joseph R. Biden and Chuck Hagel

The 2003 war on Iraq was preceded by sharp debate within the United Nations; the international body ultimately failed to endorse America and Great Britain's decision to wage war. In the following viewpoint written during that conflict, two U.S. senators, both supporters of military action against Iraq, write that the United Nations needs to be involved in securing peace and rebuilding Iraq once the fighting stops. An effort to internationalize the postwar effort to secure and rebuild Iraq would benefit not only Iraq, but the United States as well; U.S. security alliances and ties have been weakened in part because America's willingness to wage war without UN approval has caused many to question U.S. motives in Iraq, they contend. Joseph R. Biden, from Delaware, is the ranking Democrat on the Senate Foreign Relations Committee. Chuck Hagel, from Nebraska, is a Republican member of the committee.

As you read, consider the following questions:
1. How much money will the rebuilding of Iraq after the 2003 war cost, according to Biden and Hagel?
2. Why is the United Nations important in securing international support for the effort to stabilize and rebuild Iraq, according to Biden and Hagel?

Joseph R. Biden and Chuck Hagel, "Winning the Peace," *Washington Post*, April 6, 2003.

The war in Iraq is still on[1], but it's not too early to think about what the United States should do to win the peace that will follow. There may be difficult days ahead, but we are confident in the rightness of our cause, the skill of our soldiers and the certainty of our victory.

Last December [2002] we traveled to northern Iraq[2] and visited key allies in the Middle East. Nearly every leader we met stressed the importance of gaining international legitimacy for our efforts in Iraq. The best way to build such legitimacy is by involving our key allies and international organizations—starting with the United Nations—in securing and rebuilding Iraq.

Yes, our decision to use force in Iraq produced deep divisions among our Security Council allies.[3] Nonetheless, America need not and cannot take sole responsibility for the challenges of a postwar Iraq. And we must not allow the U.N. Security Council and our Atlantic allies to become casualties of war. There are five main reasons for this.

Five Reasons for International Involvement

First, building an Iraq that is secure, self-sufficient, whole and free will require tens of billions of dollars over many years. While Iraq's long-term economic promise is good, its short-term prospects are bleak. Iraq's annual oil revenue, in the first years after [the deposing of] Saddam Hussein, is projected to be no more than $15 billion. Iraq is saddled with U.N. sanctions, an estimated $61 billion in foreign debt and approximately $200 billion in reparations claims through the U.N. Compensation Commission. Experts who testified before the Senate Foreign Relations Committee put the price tag for post-conflict security, humanitarian assistance and reconstruction at $20 billion to $25 billion per

1. The 2003 war on Iraq began on March 19, 2003. President George W. Bush declared on May 1, 2003, that "major combat operations in Iraq have ended."
2. Northern Iraq was then under the control of Kurdish groups, not Saddam Hussein's regime.   3. The UN Security Council unanimously passed Resolution 1441 in November 2002, calling for Iraq to disarm or face "serious consequences." In March 2003 the United States, Great Britain, and Spain introduced a second resolution declaring that Iraq had failed to fulfill its disarmament obligations under 1441. The resolution was withdrawn without a vote in the face of opposition by many Security Council members, including France and Russia, who objected to its implicit authorization of military force against Iraq.

year over 10 years. The United States should not bear this burden alone.

Second, a military occupation, even temporary, that includes only American and British soldiers could fuel resentment throughout the Middle East, bolster [the terrorist group] al Qaeda's recruitment and make Americans a target for terrorists everywhere.

If the military mission stretches for several years, the failure to include other countries will compound these problems and turn us from liberators into occupiers. We need to make the peace in Iraq the world's responsibility, not just our own.

The Need for United Nations Leadership

Oxfam [a global confederation of antipoverty groups] believes the United Nations must play a leadership role in the immediate aftermath of the war as it has both the experience and legitimacy to help establish a representative and accountable Iraqi administration quickly. The US, UK, Australia and their allies do not.

In the short period between the end of the conflict and the establishment of an Iraqi transitional authority, Oxfam believes the UN should have full authority over civil, legal, political, economic, and humanitarian issues inside Iraq. . . .

An achievable mandate for the UN will also require the US government to fully back, both politically and financially, the United Nations, and then Iraqi authorities. If this does not happen, or the UN was perceived to be working under a US authority, the UN would be set up to fail.

"Iraq's Reconstruction and the Role of the United Nations," Oxfam policy paper, April 4, 2003.

Third, if the United States alone selects and seats a new Iraqi government, even an interim one, that will call into question the government's legitimacy in the eyes of the Iraqi people, the region and the world. Iraqis who have lived through the brutality of Hussein's rule should be given the time, space and support to choose their own leaders and to develop the institutions of a stable, representative government. We should work with other countries to help them achieve that.

Fourth, we need to place Iraq in a regional context. We

support President [George W.] Bush's commitment to restart the Middle East peace process. True security for Israel and a better future for Palestinians can be achieved only through a lasting settlement. Our "Quartet" allies—Russia, the European Union (EU) and the United Nations—have worked with us to draft a road map out of the current impasse. In addition, we need to take real steps toward a new, inclusive approach to security in the Persian Gulf that builds confidence and prevents future conflicts.

Fifth, many around the world, even longtime allies, question our motives in Iraq. They wrongly believe we are driven by commercial interests or imperial designs. We have to convince them otherwise or risk a further erosion of those alliances and institutions essential to American security and global cooperation for more than 50 years. That would undermine our interests, because it becomes increasingly difficult to contend with multiple threats to our security alone—including the unfinished war on terrorism, the dangerous nuclear programs in North Korea and Iran, and the spread of infectious diseases such as SARS. Making friends and allies who opposed the war our full partners in Iraq's peace can go a long way toward repairing the hard feelings that have emerged in recent weeks.

Internationalize the Rebuilding Effort

In short, we must internationalize our policies for rebuilding a postwar Iraq, even as we retain full control on the security side, ideally with the involvement of NATO [North Atlantic Treaty Organization], the EU and countries in the region. The best way to do that is through a new U.N. resolution authorizing the necessary security, humanitarian, reconstruction and political missions in a post-conflict Iraq.[4]

As we were told by our allies in the region in December [2002] and in subsequent meetings, securing the United Na-

4. On May 22, 2003, the United Nations Security Council passed a resolution that gave the United States and its war coalition partners a broad mandate to administer Iraq, while granting limited authority to the United Nations–appointed representative to consult with Iraqi political factions about forming a new government. The Security Council reserved the right to revisit within a year the question of who governs Iraq.

tions' endorsement would give political cover to leaders from allied countries whose people oppose the war, allowing them to justify their participation—including financial participation—in building the peace. It also would open the door to NATO, the European Union and the World Bank.

Without the United Nations, it would be difficult for governments and international organizations to buck strong public opposition and join the effort to stabilize and rebuild Iraq.

By refusing to disarm, a defiant Saddam Hussein made the fateful choice between war and peace. We must make sure that in winning the war, we also win the peace.

"*The United States and Great Britain, not the United Nations, must oversee the future of a post-Saddam Iraq.*"

America Should Limit the United Nations' Role in Rebuilding Iraq

Nile Gardiner

Unlike the 1991 Persian Gulf War, the 2003 war on Iraq that toppled the regime of Saddam Hussein was not fought under the auspices of the United Nations. However, some observers have argued that the international organization should take a leading role in administering the country after the war until a new Iraqi government is established. In the following viewpoint Nile Gardiner argues against making the United Nations responsible for governing Iraq. The organization's failure to enforce its resolutions calling for Iraqi disarmament have undermined its credibility, he contends. The countries that led the 2003 war, especially America and Great Britain, should oversee Iraq, he concludes, and the United Nations should limit its role to humanitarian projects. Gardiner is a visiting research scholar at the Heritage Foundation, a conservative public policy research institute.

As you read, consider the following questions:

1. What key war aims might be jeopardized by UN plans for a central political role in the postwar administration of Iraq, according to Gardiner?
2. What key principles does Gardiner believe should guide postwar planning for Iraq?

According to media reports, the United Nations Secretary-General's office has already drawn up detailed plans for the UN to step in and administer Iraq three months after the war is over.[1] The confidential blueprint calls for a UN Assistance Mission to be established in Baghdad, which would oversee a post-Saddam [Hussein] Iraqi government.

It is imperative that . . . the Bush Administration rebuff UN plans for a central role in a post-war government. Such a plan would jeopardize the United States' key war aims, including the:

- Hunt for weapons of mass destruction and terrorist cells;
- Protection of Iraq's energy infrastructure;
- Securing of large cities;
- Defense of Iraq's borders; and
- Protection of Kurdish areas.

It would also seriously hamper President [George W.] Bush's vision of establishing a free Iraqi nation from the ashes of tyranny, and spreading democracy throughout the Middle East.

An organization that failed to enforce no less than 17 resolutions calling for Iraqi disarmament lacks the moral standing or the capability to either administer Iraq or to enforce security in the country after Saddam Hussein is removed from power. There is an important role to be played by the United Nations in a post-war Iraq—but it should be limited and restricted to purely humanitarian intervention, carried out by agencies such as UNICEF and the World Food Program.

The Bush Administration Plans for Post-War Iraq

In a statement to Congress on March 26 [2003], Secretary of State Colin Powell made it clear that Washington would not give the United Nations a commanding role in administering a post-war Iraq, saying, "We didn't take on this huge burden with our coalition partners not to be able to have a significant dominating control over how it unfolds in the future." Powell's comments have echoed remarks made by White House and Pentagon officials who have expressed

1. According to an account in the March 5, 2003, edition of the London *Times*, plans were drawn up in February 2003 while military action against Iraq was still being debated. America and Great Britain launched attacks on Iraq on March 19, 2003.

doubts about a post-war role for the UN.

The Bush Administration envisages a temporary U.S.-led administration, which will govern Iraq for a period of several months until an interim Iraqi government can be put in place. . . . The administration will be charged with overseeing civil governance, reconstruction, and humanitarian assistance.

The UN as a Trojan Horse

In the coming weeks [April and May 2003], the United States will face mounting pressure from other members of the UN Security Council, most notably France, Russia and Germany, to cede control of a post-war administration to the UN. France's Foreign Minister, Dominique de Villepin, has argued that the UN must have supremacy in post-war Baghdad, saying "The UN must steer the process and must be at the heart of the reconstruction and administration of Iraq."

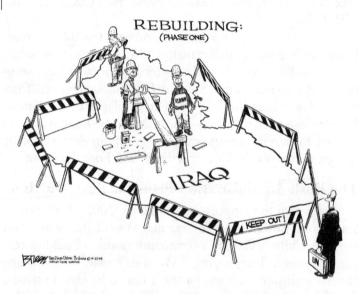

Breen. © 2003 by *San Diego Union-Tribune*. Reprinted by permission of Copley News Service.

In a sharp riposte to British Prime Minister Tony Blair, the three aforementioned nations have stipulated that a UN mandate for a post-Saddam government will only be given on their terms. French President Jacques Chirac has made it clear that France will veto any resolution at the UN Security Council that "would legitimize the military intervention and give the belligerents, the United States and the United Kingdom, the right to administer Iraq."

The Paris-Moscow-Berlin axis has unequivocally condemned U.S.-British military action against the Iraqi regime, and has refused to cooperate with London and Washington by not expelling Iraqi diplomats from their capitals. A UN-controlled post-war administration would merely serve as a Trojan horse for European nations opposed to regime change, enabling them to stake their economic and strategic claims in Iraq.

The spectacle of French or Russian bureaucrats, who for decades have tried to keep a brutal dictator in power, ruling over the Iraqi people, would be utterly abhorrent. It is important for the future of Iraq's citizens that Paris, Moscow and Berlin play no significant part in the creation of the new Iraqi state.

Key Principles That Should Be Applied

The Bush Administration should apply the following guidelines in relation to the UN and the international community in planning for a post-war Iraq.

- The United States and Great Britain, not the United Nations, must oversee the future of a post-Saddam Iraq. There is no need for a UN resolution mandating a post-war Allied administration.
- The role of the United Nations in a post-war Iraq should be purely humanitarian.
- Only those nations that have joined the 'coalition of the willing' should participate in the post-war administration and security of Iraq.
- Oil and other financial contracts signed between Saddam Hussein's regime and European governments and companies which have violated international law should not be honored by the post-war government.
- There must be a full and exhaustive investigation into links between French, German and Russian companies and politicians, and the Iraqi dictatorship, once the

Baathist regime's archives have been opened in Baghdad. U.S. sanctions should be applied against any nation that contributed to Iraq's development of weapons of mass destruction or violated the UN oil for food program.

A Dying Force

The United Nations is slowly dying as a force on the world stage, and will go the same way as the League of Nations unless it is radically reformed and restructured. It failed spectacularly to deal with the growing threat posed by Saddam Hussein, and its influence is likely to diminish further in the coming years.

Against this backdrop, President Bush should make it clear that there is no need for further discussions on the Iraq issue at the UN. Indeed, the role of the United Nations in a post-war Iraq should be limited to purely humanitarian involvement. The UN should play a subordinate role on the Iraq question, with the United States and Great Britain taking the lead in administering a post-war Iraqi transition government. UN intervention in a post-Saddam Iraq would merely strengthen the hand of those nations who have opposed even the principle of regime change in Baghdad, and which have appeased the Iraqi dictatorship for decades.

Periodical Bibliography

The following articles have been selected to supplement the diverse views presented in this chapter.

Frederick D. Barton and Bathsheba Crocker	"Winning the Peace in Iraq," *Washington Quarterly*, Spring 2003.
Peter Beinart	"TRB from Washington: Free Form," *New Republic*, May 5, 2003.
Carl Bildt	"Hard-Earned Lessons on Nation-Building: Seven Ways to Rebuild Iraq," *International Herald Tribune*, May 7, 2003.
Patrick J. Buchanan	"The Wages of Empire," *Los Angeles Times*, February 23, 2003.
Adeed Dawisha and Karen Dawisha	"How to Build a Democratic Iraq," *Foreign Affairs*, May/June 2003.
Thomas Donnelly	"There's No Place Like Iraq . . . " *Weekly Standard*, May 5, 2003.
John W. Dower	"Lessons from Japan About War's Aftermath," *New York Times*, October 27, 2002.
Bilal El-Amine	"Gunboat Democracy," *Left Turn*, May/June 2003.
James Fallows	"The Fifty-first State?" *Atlantic Monthly*, November 2002.
John Gray	"Unfit for the Burdens of Empire," *New Statesman*, April 21, 2003.
Andrew Greeley	"U.S. Miscalculates in Iraq," *Chicago Sun-Times*, May 2, 2003.
John B. Judis	"A Case for Hell," *American Prospect*, April 2003.
Joe Klein	"To Remake Iraq, Invite the Neighbors Over," *Time*, May 5, 2003.
Rami G. Khouri	"Getting It Right in Iraq," *Maclean's*, May 19, 2003.
Stanley Kurtz	"Democratic Imperialism: A Blueprint," *Policy Review*, April 2003.
Los Angeles Times	"Iraq Mire Is a Global Issue," September 4, 2003.
Richard Lugar	"A Victory at Risk," *Washington Post*, May 22, 2003.
New York Times	"A Bigger U.N. Role in Iraq," September 4, 2003.

Ralph Peters	"Still Not Enough Troops," *New York Post*, May 14, 2003.
Stuart Taylor Jr.	"The U.N. Is Often Grotesque, but We Need Its Help," *National Journal*, April 26, 2003.
Fareed Zakaria	"How to Make Friends in Iraq," *Newsweek*, June 23, 2003.
Fareed Zakaria	"What We Should Do Now," *Newsweek*, September 1, 2003.

CHAPTER 3

What Kind of Government Should Iraq Have?

Chapter Preface

The end of Saddam Hussein's regime in April 2003 following the U.S.-led military invasion of Iraq left the country in a political state of flux and under temporary American occupation. It also raised the question of what kind of government Iraq could and should create to ultimately take authority from its American occupiers. American military occupation helped create democratic governments in Germany and Japan following World War II, but some observers have questioned whether such a feat can be repeated in Iraq. Two of their main concerns are the social legacy of Hussein's rule and the influence of Islam.

During his more than two decades as ruler of Iraq, Hussein maintained tight control over his country; kept political power in the hands of family members and trusted subordinates; and jailed, tortured, and killed political opponents. Iraqis' long history as an oppressed people may hinder the development of democracy in the region, some observers believe. People in a totalitarian regime "lose the habits of citizenship," argues writer David Brooks. "Individuals . . . can't be sure that even their own family members won't betray them. They fall into a passivity induced by the impossibility of freedom." Such habits of passivity and receptivity to authoritarian rulers may be hard to break, he concludes, and may make it more difficult for Iraq to create a functioning democracy.

Another reason many observers are skeptical of Iraq's democratic future is the role of Islam in that nation. The demise of Hussein's Baath Party regime in 2003 left a power vacuum that quickly began to be filled by Muslim clerical leaders, many of whom voiced opposition to Western secular democracy (and continued American occupation). Since Shiites—Arab Muslims who follow the Shiite branch of Islam—constitute 60 percent of Iraq's people, a national election may conceivably result in the creation of an Islamic theocracy similar to the one that has ruled Iran since 1979. Such a development may be welcomed by many of Iraq's Shiites, who have suffered under Hussein and who believe that an Islamic form of government is in Iraq's best interests. But Iran's government has been condemned by many throughout the world for its oppression and violation of human rights, and many, both within and outside Iraq, find the prospect of a Iran-style Islamic regime alarming.

Not everyone is pessimistic about Iraq's prospects for democracy, arguing that Iraq's high literacy rate, oil wealth, and other assets may help its transition to a representative form of government. Optimists include President George W. Bush, who in an April 2003 speech asserted that "the Iraqi people are fully capable of self-government" and that "every day, Iraqis are moving toward democracy and embracing the responsibilities of active citizenship." The viewpoints in this chapter present various views on what kind of government Iraq should have.

"*Iraq can become peaceful, secular and democratic—a beacon of hope in the Middle East.*"

Iraq Should Have a Secular Democracy

Barham Salih

Barham Salih is prime minister of the Patriotic Union of Kurdistan (PUK), one of two Kurdish groups that were able in the 1990s to establish autonomous local governments in northern Iraq outside the control of Saddam Hussein. The PUK cooperated with Americans in the 2003 war that deposed Saddam Hussein—a conflict that began shortly after the following viewpoint was first published. In it Salih welcomes U.S. intervention to overthrow Hussein but argues that such use of force will only be deemed a triumph if it helps to create a secular and democratic regime in Iraq. A successful transition to democracy requires the participation of both Iraqi exile organizations and indigenous political groups. The experiences of the Kurds in creating a regional government show that creating a secular democracy is possible in Iraq, Salih concludes.

As you read, consider the following questions:
1. Why does the author consider war against Saddam Hussein to be the only option for the Iraqi people?
2. What does the author mean by "de-Baathification" and why does he consider it to be important?
3. What warning does Salih issue regarding Iraq's neighbors, Iran and Turkey?

No one wants a war in Iraq less than the Iraqi people. But we don't have the luxury of being anti-war. For the past 35 years, the Baathist regime has been waging war against Iraqis. We know there can be no peace without the military liberation of Iraq. The brutality of Saddam Hussein's regime leaves Iraqis and the civilised world with no other option.

And so, not for the first time, a persecuted people is asking for help in dislodging a dictatorship. But we also ask that the United States protect and nurture a postwar Iraqi democracy. The [2003] US-led campaign must be about more than simply eliminating weapons of mass destruction and forcing a regime change. Rather, the use of force must yield a clear political gain: the foundation of a democratic state that will be at peace with its own people and with the Middle East.

It is too often forgotten that Iraq is the ultimate failed state, the twisted product of British colonialism. From its beginning, the Iraqi state brutalised its Kurdish minority and excluded the Shiite majority. Although uniquely brutal, the present Baath dictatorship is also a symptom of the closely interwoven political and military structures that evolved from the colonial era. With little base of support, Baghdad regularly used force to impose its will.

Transition to Democracy

The transition from the status quo to a democratic state is a process in which the US and the international community will have to play a pivotal role. The US-led coalition will be instrumental in getting rid of dictatorship. And the US military will undoubtedly be central to stabilising the security environment and offering the Iraqis the space within which they can develop a democratic system.

But peace in postwar Iraq, much less democracy, cannot be established without the full participation of the nation's secular democratic movements and other indigenous political groups. Iraq has a long history of political and social opposition to the Baath regime, and the regime's diverse opponents will all want to play a role in shaping a postwar Iraq.

A national transitional authority, drawing from these domestic political movements and aided by the US-led coalition and the United Nations, must be quickly put into place [after Saddam Hussein is deposed]. A delay in handing over power to a national authority will play into the hands of undemocratic anti-Western forces, not only in Iraq, but in the wider Islamic world.

De-Baathification

During the transition period, de-Baathification (like de-Nazification in the period after World War II) will be a vitally important, if complicated, undertaking. As a first step, the regime's much feared security services must be dismantled. The military must be demobilised to facilitate the purging of Baathists and human rights violators, and then restructured to serve the peace and security of the people. The highly centralised Baath structures control the political, economic and social spheres of Iraq and must be dismantled. New decentralised and accountable institutions must be set in place.

Separation of Church and State

Secular governments best promote the twin goals of religious liberty and social stability.

In the aftermath of decades of Baathist repression, the risk of religious strife in postwar Iraq is considerable. In addition to ethnic diversity, there are significant divisions between and within Sunni and Shia Islamic groups, not to mention Christian and other minorities. Some commentators thus suggest that Iraq is not fertile soil for the transplant of American political ideals. . . .

Nevertheless, it was precisely the experience of religious repression and sectarian strife in Europe and the American colonies that encouraged Baptist leaders such as Roger Williams and John Leland to promote the separation of church and state. This American principle emerged and gradually gained support from religious and political leaders in difficult and uncertain times, not an era of tranquility and stability.

K. Hollyn Hollman, *Church-State Intersection*, April 2003.

De-Baathification also means reforming the economy. State control and centralisation foster corruption while millions live in poverty. The oil industry needs to be de-monopolised and its revenues devoted to the well-being of the population and the economic revival of the country.

Within the structures that maintain the Baath dictatorship lies a deeper problem. What Iraqis call a Baath mentality permeates the educational system, warps social services and dominates a greatly weakened civil society. A 35-year process of Baathification has inculcated the norms and values that bolster the dictatorship into every nook and cranny of society. The Baath mentality values obedience over initiative, deference to authority over critical thinking, loyalty over ability and violence over conflict resolution.

This Baath mentality will take a while to eradicate, but the process must begin immediately. This will require reforming the educational systems and establishing methods of identifying and rewarding talent, merit, ability, independent thinking and service to the community in new institutions.

A vigorous truth and reconciliation process must be instituted to begin to heal the wounds and instil a sense of justice among the people. The leadership of the Baath party must be tried for war crimes and crimes against humanity. The 40-year "ethnic-cleansing" campaign that has displaced hundreds of thousands of Kurds, Turkomans and Assyrian Christians from Kirkuk, Khanaqin and Sinjar must be reversed.

The transitional authority must organise and hold elections for a constituent assembly, preferably within a year. This will give the people of Iraq a personal stake in the success of a new government.

This transition process will be greatly complicated if neighbouring countries attempt to intervene militarily. The presence of regional troops in Iraq may open a Pandora's box of historical sensitivities. . . .

Kurdistan's Example

The anticipated difficulties with regime change and peaceful transition would be exacerbated by the involvement of neighbouring countries. Iran and Turkey, and for that matter other neighbours, have much to gain from a stable, peaceful Iraq. Their military involvement is not needed and would be counterproductive. If the US wants to avoid a quagmire in Iraq, it will keep the focus on Iraq and will keep the neighbours at bay. Eleven years ago [in 1992], the people of Iraqi Kurdistan embarked on pioneering experiments in democratic self-government in the heart of the Islamic Middle East. The success of the Kurdistan Regional Government stands to prove that Iraq need not be ruled by tyranny and illustrates that despite all the impediments, democracy in Iraq is possible.

With international assistance, Iraq can become a country its citizens will want to live in because it will offer individual rights, political freedom and economic opportunity. It can become a country that stands for peace over aggression and terrorism, democracy over dictatorship, secularism over theocracy and economic prosperity.

None of this will be easy, but doing nothing will ultimately prove more costly. With the US by our side, Iraq can become peaceful, secular and democratic—a beacon of hope in the Middle East.

I"Muslims don't want secularism."

The Iraqi People Do Not Want a Secular Democracy

Amir Butler

Amir Butler is executive director of the Australian Muslim Public Affairs Committee. In the following viewpoint, which Butler wrote during America's 2003 war with Iraq, he questions whether the United States really intends to have Iraqis control their own political future. He contends that the majority of Iraq's people, like most Middle Easterners, seek a greater role for the Islamic religion in political affairs, and that many object to regional governments (including Saddam Hussein's regime) because they are too secular. American designs to make Iraq a secular democracy fail to take into account the fact that Iraq's people do not want such a government, according to Butler.

As you read, consider the following questions:

1. What parallels does Butler draw between American actions in 2003 and British actions following World War I?
2. What test does the author propose to determine if the United States is sincere in its statements about liberating the people of the Middle East?
3. What central schism accounts for political violence and repression in the Middle East, according to Butler?

Baghdad will fall within days. Saddam will be killed, the Iraqi army routed, and the Ba'ath Party relegated to the garbage bin of history. Democracy will bloom, and peace and tranquility will descend on Iraq, and then the entire Middle East. Muslim radicals will transform en masse into social democrats. There will be no more war or terrorism, and everyone will live happily ever after. Even the mothers of children whose limbs have been blown off by allied cluster bombs will, in the words of the British Defence Secretary, "one day" thank Britain for their use. So goes the chimerical script plotted by the Bush administration and their coterie of neo-conservative advisors.

However, like so many an American production, Gulf War II[1] is a re-run of a British classic. Almost 85 years to the day when Tommy Franks[2] spoke of "liberating" Iraq and not conquering it, the British Lt General Stanley Maude had assured the people of Iraq: "Our armies do not come into your cities and lands as conquerors or enemies, but as liberators".[3]

For the Iraqis of the early 20th century, "liberty through occupation" meant having their country carved up, a puppet regime put in place, buttressed by British military might, followed by years of bloody rebellion. The Arabs killed 450 British soldiers and wounded 2,000. The British deployed 90,000 soldiers to liberate the country and ended up liberating over 10,000 Arab souls from their bodies. In an irony typical of so much in our history, the British used the weapons of mass destruction (poison gas) of their day against the Iraqi resistance fighters.

Now it's all being repeated again: the same language; the same bravado; the same promises of "liberation" and "democracy"; the same lies; and the same descent into violent chaos.

The Litmus Test

Is America any more sincere in its objective of "freeing" the Middle East than the British were in "freeing" Iraq from the

1. the 2003 military action by the United States and Great Britain that deposed Saddam Hussein   2. U.S. general and supreme commander of the coalition forces that invaded Iraq in 2003   3. The quote is taken from Maude's "Proclamation to the People of the Wilayat of Baghdad," issued on March 8, 1917. Maude commanded a British force that invaded Iraq, then part of the Turkish Ottoman Empire, during World War I.

Turks during World War I? Here's the litmus test: When America articulates its vision for the Middle East of regimes falling and "democracies" appearing in their place, is it also willing to accept that these democracies may not be secular and may not be as malleable to American interests as the previous regimes? In other words, does America also recognize the right of the people to decide their own system of government and elect the governments that they, the people, want?

Choosing Islam over Democracy

Muslims and Arabs neither will accept nor embrace democracy if they believe that it is foreign or alien to Islam. To those who continue to insist that Islam and democracy are not compatible, let me offer this pragmatic approach: Muslims see Islam not just as their religion, but also as their identity and culture. Some people want to promote democracy in the Muslim world by telling them: "We have this wonderful product for you. It's called democracy. It will solve all your problems. It will take care of your political, economic and social problems. It will cure your governance ills and give you prosperity. There's just one problem: It is not compatible with your religion. You have to choose either democracy or Islam." Take a guess which one they will choose!

Abdulwahab Alksebi, *Insight on the News*, April 1, 2003.

I think not. This war is not being fought to give the Muslim world the kind of freedom that, when sincerely exercised, will bring into being governments that may oppose American interests or may actually reflect popular anger on the Palestinian issue.

Yet, clearly, the Muslim world is in need of some change. Almost all of the countries are ruled by despotic dictatorships hated by their constituents. Whilst we are amongst the richest societies, we have amongst the lowest levels of literacy and are plagued with intellectual, political and economic stagnation. Political violence and unrest are features of almost all.

However, the idea that the export of secular democracy to the Muslim world at the barrel of a gun will solve the Muslim world's problems is completely detached from the realities of Muslim society.

The reality is that most all Muslim countries are already secular. Nobody can doubt the secular credentials of a country like Egypt where wearing a beard and praying your morning prayers in a mosque can be an invitation for security forces to harass you, or a country like Turkey where women are banned from graduating from university if they wear a scarf.

The Schism in the Muslim World

At the same time as governments and the elites of the Muslim world are staunchly secular, the common people are not. It is this schism between the leaders of the Muslim world and their constituents that forms the sociological basis for most of the political violence that blights the Muslim world. In Egypt, for example, the violence of the al-Jamaahal-Islamiyyah organization (whose leaders went on to become ideological powerhouses of [the terrorist network] al-Qaeda) was a reaction to the extremist violence of the Nasser regime. When Muslim activists began peacefully calling for an increased role for religion in the state, the Arab nationalist Gamel Abdel Nasser[4] initiated a program of imprisonment, forced disappearance and torture to quell dissent. The reaction of the people was violence directed at the state, which escalated into a cycle of violence that continues to this day in the form of assassination of tourists and government employees.

Likewise, the civil war in Algeria that left thousands dead was a result of the government's intervention in the country's first ever free election [in 1997]. When it became apparent that Islamic parties looked set to win, the government cancelled the election. With democracy suspended, the people rebelled and the country was plunged into a civil war that left thousands dead. . . .

That extreme behaviour by a government begets extreme behavior from its constituents is a truism that the American government should consider as its centurions march across the Middle East and its bombs fall on Arab cities.

Muslims are increasingly asking for Islam to play a role in the affairs of the state and for governments that actually rep-

4. the military ruler of Egypt from 1952 to 1970

resent the interests of their constituents rather than "bunker regimes" that view their constituents as an enemy. If America thinks that imposing, at the barrel of the gun, American-backed secular regimes in place of the current secular regimes is going to lead to some sort of Muslim Enlightenment, then it is dangerously wrong. Muslims don't want secularism and to be subjects of some Arab Quisling; they want and will fight for true democracy and freedom to choose their own systems of government. And when George W. Bush promises "freedom" to the Muslim people, this is definitely not the type of freedom he means.

> "Iraq needs—and I write these words with some trepidation—a democratically-minded Iraqi strongman."

Iraq Needs Transitional Rule by a Strongman

Daniel Pipes

Daniel Pipes is the director of the Middle East Forum, a think tank that works to define and promote American interests in the Middle East. He has also written numerous books and articles on the region. In the following viewpoint written shortly after Saddam Hussein was deposed in 2003 by American-led coalition troops, Pipes argues that Iraq is in danger of falling under the control of a militant Islamic regime similar to the one governing Iraq's neighbor, Iran. Such an outcome, he contends, must be prevented. He proposes that a "strongman" be installed by the U.S.-led coalition to rule Iraq in the interim to maintain stability and prevent an Islamic takeover. He adds that the United States and its coalition partners should maintain a quiet and supportive presence in the nation and help Iraqis plan a gradual transition to a democratic government.

As you read, consider the following questions:
1. In what bind does the United States and its allies find themselves, according to Pipes?
2. What two pieces of advice does the author provide?
3. What social infrastructure is necessary before elections can be held, according to Pipes?

Thousands of Iraqi Shi'ites chanted "No to America, No to Saddam, Yes to Islam" a few days ago [in April 2003], during pilgrimage rites at the holy city of Karbala. Increasing numbers of Iraqis appear to agree with these sentiments. They have ominous implications for the coalition forces.[1]

Gratitude for liberation usually has a short shelf life, and Iraq will be no exception. As a middle-aged factory manager put it, "Thank you, Americans. But now we don't need anybody to stay here anymore."

However delighted they are to be rid of the Saddamite nightmare, Iraqis mentally live in a world of conspiracy theories, causing many to harbor deep suspicions of coalition intentions.

"Yes to Islam" in effect means "Yes to Iranian-style militant Islam." The introduction of that failed system would be a disaster for Iraq and would revive the Khomeini[2] message which by now has lost nearly all appeal in Iran.

A Bind

This state of affairs leaves coalition forces in a bind: As vanquisher of the Saddam Hussein regime, they aim to rehabilitate the country, which means sticking around. As liberator of the country, they must respond to Iraqi wishes, which means getting out fast.

What to do? If coalition forces leave Iraq precipitously, anarchy and extremism would result. Stay too long, they will face an anti-imperialist backlash of sabotage and terrorism. Hold elections too fast, the Khomeini-like mullahs will probably win. Keep the country under an occupation force, and an intifada would rear up.

The U.S. and U.K. governments need to square the circle—put the country to right while getting out of the way, and bring about democracy without letting the Iranians take over. I offer two pieces of advice:

- *Plan for the long haul.* Building a full democracy (meaning, regularly voting the head of government out of of-

1. The United States led an international coalition that invaded Iraq and overthrew Saddam Hussein in April 2003. Most of the coalition troops were from the United States and Great Britain.   2. Ayatollah Ruhollah Khomeini, a Muslim cleric, led a political revolution in Iran in 1979 that created an Islamic government.

fice) takes time. From the Magna Carta in 1215 to the Reform Act of 1832, England needed six centuries. The United States needed over a century. Things have sped up these days, but it still takes twenty or more years to reach full democracy. That was the timetable in countries as varied as South Korea, Chile, Poland and Turkey.

• *Plan for a gradual transition.* A population emerging from thirty years in the dungeon cannot cope with all the choices of full democracy, but must get there in steps. Democratically-minded autocrats can guide the country to full democracy better than snap elections.

The Paradox of Occupation

The next few years [after the Iraq War of 2003] are crucial, because it is during this same period that a constitution must be written, power sharing must begin, courts must be established and important policy decisions about oil and rebuilding must be taken. The United States will have to get involved in these decisions to ensure that they are not hijacked by one group or another in Iraq. Until a legitimate Iraqi government has been formed—until national elections—the United States will play the role of honest broker among the various factions.

And yet this is going to be called colonialism. The Iraqis who feel excluded from the new regime will level that charge instantly. Others in the Arab world who are threatened by the changes in Iraq will want Iraq to slip back into "normalcy"— which is to say dictatorship. The Saudi foreign minister called . . . for an end to the "occupation" of Iraq—before Baghdad had even fallen into American hands. This then is the paradox: to build democracy in Iraq the United States must stay on, but to demonstrate that it is not a colonial power it must leave.

Fareed Zakaria, *Newsweek*, April 21, 2003.

Therefore: Iraq needs—and I write these words with some trepidation—a democratically-minded Iraqi strongman. This may sound like a contradiction, but it has happened elsewhere, for example by Atatürk in Turkey and Chiang Kai-shek in Taiwan. Yes, it goes against every American instinct ("Democracy Now!" is the name of a national radio show) but that's not a reason to reject it.

Democracy is a learned habit, not instinct. The infrastructure of a civil society—such as freedom of speech, freedom of movement, freedom of assembly, the rule of law, minority rights and an independent judiciary—needs to be established before holding elections. Deep attitudinal changes must take place as well: a culture of restraint, a commonality of values, a respect for differences of view and a sense of civic responsibility.

Such institutions and views will need years to grow in Iraq. In the meantime, elections should begin on the local level. The press should inch toward full freedom, political parties should grow organically, parliament should gain in authority. The Shi'ites can develop democratic ideas, uninfluenced by Khomeinism.

Who should fill the all-important role of strongman? The ideal candidate would be politically moderate but operationally tough; someone with an ambition to steer Iraq toward democracy and good neighborly relations.

As for the coalition forces, after installing a strongman they should phase out their visible role and pull back to a few military bases away from population centers. From these, they can quietly serve as the military partner of the new government, guaranteeing its ultimate security and serving as a constructive influence for the entire region.

The approach outlined here undercuts the rage of anti-imperialism, finesses the almost certain violence against coalition troops and prevents the Iranians from colonizing Iraq. But the window of opportunity is closing rapidly: Unless the coalition appoints a strongman very soon, it will not achieve its ambitious goals.

"The last thing Iraqis need is another strongman."

Iraq Needs a Transitional Government with Dispersed Powers

Laith Kubba

The following viewpoint by Iraqi political activist Laith Kubba was written a few months before the 2003 war that ended the regime of Saddam Hussein. In it he argues that the formation of a democratic government in Iraq will be a difficult but not impossible task and outlines a series of steps to follow in creating an interim government. He rejects the notion that Iraq needs a temporary dictator or strongman to maintain order in a post-Saddam Iraq. Instead, Kubba recommends the establishment of an interim government of three separate councils with well-defined powers and responsibilities, overseen by a three-member presidency. Power should be shared by Iraqi military officers and leading opposition groups. Kubba is a founding member of the Iraqi National Congress, an umbrella group of Iraqi exile organizations.

As you read, consider the following questions:
1. How quickly must an Iraqi interim regime be created, according to Kubba?
2. What are the main roles to be performed by the three temporary councils proposed by Kubba?
3. What are the main advantages the author claims for his proposed plan of the transition process?

S ooner or later, there will be a regime change in Iraq.[1] Yet neither the US government, the international community nor the Iraqi opposition has agreed [on] a plan for the "day after". None of the options that have been suggested so far is workable. One is a government in exile. Yet Iraqi exiles are too divided among themselves and do not command loyalty inside Iraq. Another option is an interim military regime. But this would have little public support and would be vulnerable to civilian insurrection and armed insurgency.

The uncertainty clouding Iraq's future is helping the tyranny of Saddam Hussein by fuelling doubt, fear and hesitation about what to do next among both European countries and Iraq's neighbours.

Can Iraq's polarised communities of Shi'ites, Kurds and Sunnis or its fragmented opposition groups transform their battered country, establishing a stable constitutional order after decades of war and brutal dictatorship? The answer, fortunately, is yes. The leaders of a post-Saddam Iraq must tackle a series of difficult but by no means impossible transitional tasks. What is needed is an inclusive form of interim administration that can maintain order and restore public services while allowing all interest groups to air their views about the country's future.

Specifically, they must: create a constitutional assembly with a coherent agenda; hold a free and fair referendum on ratification; and, ultimately, seek power through the ballot box. The real challenge will be to do all this relatively quickly—say, within a year—while maintaining law and order and meeting urgent humanitarian needs.

Three Councils

No one person, group, or coalition has the authority, legitimacy or power to lead Iraq during transition. Moreover, the last thing Iraqis need is another strongman. To accomplish what it needs, Iraq's interim administration should have three temporary councils, each with a well-defined set of powers and responsibilities.

---

1. This article was published a few months before Iraqi leader Saddam Hussein was deposed in April 2003 by a U.S.-led military invasion.

The first would function as a lower house for deputies appointed or elected by political groups. Opposition formations, whether in exile or northern Iraq, could fill up to three-quarters of its 200 seats, the rest going to groups now based within Iraq.

Lane. © 2003 by *Baltimore Sun*. Reprinted with permission.

The second council would be a sort of senate, with 100 seats mainly for tribal, religious, and ethnic dignitaries. It would give traditional leaders a role without requiring them to politicise their communal identities. It would also ensure the inclusion of minorities such as Turkmens and Chaldean and Assyrian Christians. In addition to offering Iraqis a forum for political bargaining, these two councils would play a direct role in nominating members of the constitutional assembly, setting its agenda, and approving the draft constitution that it produces before this goes to the voters. To forestall conflict over executive power during the transition, the bureaucracy should be kept out of the hands of political groups and armed organisations. Likewise, the interim political councils should stay out of administrative matters.

A third council would look after national security. Its mission would be to secure the borders, stop violent conflicts, and assert control over weapons and armed men so citizens need not fear assault or the outbreak of private warfare. Such a council would have to include selected officers from the current Iraqi military and security establishment and representatives of the Kurdistan Democratic Party (KDP), the Patriotic Union of Kurdistan (PUK), and the Shi'ite Supreme Council of the Islamic Revolution in Iraq (SCIRI), which between them field tens of thousands of armed fighters. To ensure the unbroken provision of vital public services, the interim government should let most of Saddam's ordinary civilian bureaucrats, as opposed to secret police and other henchmen, keep their jobs.

Overseeing the entire transition process would be a three-member presidency with sovereign authority over the three temporary councils. The presidency would comprise one senior figure each from the north, the centre and the south. Each of these members must have an untarnished record of integrity and public service to Iraq.

The presidency should have power to appoint cabinet ministers, approve nominations of additional members to the temporary councils, and ensure the legitimacy of the procedures of the constitutional assembly. The presidency members should consult with the KDP and PUK regarding any nominations concerning the north, and with the SCIRI regarding the south.

Compromises Are Necessary

Inevitably, this plan is only an outline. It will not please everyone. But these shortcomings are outweighed by its virtues. It accommodates many players without allowing them to undermine the transition. It allows a legitimate and legal transfer of power. It provides for a transitional administration that can serve the Iraqi people rather than fractious political groups. The plan makes Iraq's existing armed groups part of the solution to disorder rather than part of the problem.

For this plan to work, all Iraqi groups need to understand that their interest lies in a peaceful transition. That will only succeed if they are prepared to compromise. There will always be forces that will want to upset the chessboard if they cannot win every time. But a new game with new rules would allow the Iraqi people to take their destiny into their own hands and lay the groundwork for a peaceful and democratic future.

"Iraqis are not likely to leave Islam in a drawer at home as they gather to form their government."

The United States Should Permit Iraqis to Elect an Islamic Regime

Joan Ryan

After the United States led a military coalition that over-threw Iraqi dictator Saddam Hussein in April 2003, U.S. officials indicated that American forces would remain to help rebuild Iraq and create a democratic government. In the following viewpoint Joan Ryan argues that Americans must be prepared for the creation of an Islam-based government in Iraq, a country in which Muslims constitute 95 percent of the population. Most Muslims, she contends, do not believe in the separation between religion and politics and would support a government with strong Islamic elements. While many Americans might find the prospect of such a government disturbing, the United States cannot proclaim its support for democracy while dictating to the Iraqi people what kind of government they can have. Ryan is a columnist for the *San Francisco Chronicle*.

As you read, consider the following questions:

1. What reaction does Ryan have to the fall of Saddam Hussein?
2. Why do Muslims in the Arab world not believe in the separation of church and state, according to the author?
3. What lessons does Ryan draw from the experiences of Turkey in creating a secular government?

There is nothing more stirringly symbolic of a new political era than the statue of a conquered leader toppling from its pedestal. Even those of us who oppose the [2003] war in Iraq couldn't help but rejoice with the Iraqi men who looped wire and rope around Saddam Hussein's statue in Baghdad.

As one friend said, freeing the Iraqis from Hussein's tyranny is the silver lining in this mushroom cloud.

Now, we just have to help the folks form a democratic government and, presto change-o, our work is done.

I don't mean to be flippant, because nothing could be more serious than ushering in a new way of life for a repressed people. But there's a sense here in the United States that, given half a chance, democracy will burst forth like song from any collection of human beings. Perhaps this is correct.

Different Ideas

But the Iraqis' idea of democracy might be quite different from our own.

U.S. National Security Adviser Condoleezza Rice assured reporters . . . that the new government "will be broad-based, drawing from all of Iraq's religious and ethnic groups, including Iraqis inside and outside of Iraq. It will be a means for Iraqis to participate immediately in the economic and political reconstruction of their country."

In other words, they will decide for themselves who their leaders will be and what their government will look like. If you're a liberator, this is the one drawback to democracy. You cannot "install" a democracy. If you did, of course, the resulting government would not be a democracy. There cannot be democracy without independence.

So the American public has to be prepared to accept that the Iraqis' choice of leaders—indeed, their very interpretation of democracy—might not be what we had in mind. One aspect in particular might be especially disturbing to Americans: Iraqis are not likely to leave Islam in a drawer at home as they gather to form their government.

The separation of church and state is alien to Islamic history. For many—if not most—Muslims in the Arab world, the divine and the secular are one. They do not compartmental-

The United States, Iraq, and Democracy

America is a friend to the talented people of Iraq and to their aspirations. Our demands are directed only at the regime that enslaves them and threatens the rest of the world. Freed from the weight of oppression, Iraqis will be able to share in the progress and prosperity of our time. The United States and our allies are prepared to help the Iraqi people create the institutions of liberty in a free and unified Iraq.

Some will argue that the United States is prepared only to support electoral outcomes that please Washington. This is not so. The United States will support democratic processes even if those empowered do not choose policies to our liking. But let me be clear on this point. U.S. relations with governments, even if fairly elected, will depend on how they treat their own people, and on how they act on the international stage on issues ranging from terrorism to trade and non-proliferation to narcotics.

In promoting democracy, we are well aware that a sudden move toward open elections in Muslim-majority countries could bring Islamist parties to power. The reason, however, is not because Islamist parties enjoy the overwhelming confidence of the population, but because they are often the only organized opposition to a status quo that growing numbers of people find unacceptable. That said, let there be no misunderstanding: the United States is not opposed to Muslim parties, just as we are not opposed to Christian, Jewish or Hindu parties in democracies with broad foundations.

Richard N. Haass, U.S. Department of State, remarks to the Council on Foreign Relations, December 4, 2002.

ize; for them, Islam predominates over every human activity.

"If we understand democracy as a form of government that is respective of and responsive to the wishes of the majority of the people, then some form of 'Islamicity' is going to be part of the new government," said Hamid Algar, who has been a professor of Islamic studies at UC Berkeley for more than 30 years.

Islam and Democracy

Islam is so interwoven into the daily lives of Muslims that banishing it from political life is not possible, Algar said.

"From that point of view," he said, "one can say secularism is in fact a contradiction with democracy in an Islamic context."

Algar is among those who argue that even Turkey, which has been a democracy since Kemal Ataturk founded the Turkish Republic in 1923, still struggles with unresolved issues of church and state. It is not a neat separation. The government forbids the free expression of one's religious affiliation by banning all religious symbols from public life. It bans women who wear traditional headscarves called hejabs from entering public universities and government offices.

Turkey is considered the most successful democracy among Islamic countries, but the tension between the secular and the religious factions has undermined valued tenets of democracy. The Turkish army has staged three coups between 1960 and 1980 to push out leaders it disapproved of, banned political parties, and jailed activists who strayed too far from Ataturk's principles.

There is no blueprint for Iraq to follow in rebuilding its government. America has much guidance to offer, having sustained a thriving democracy for more than 200 years. But in the end, we must keep our word. The Iraqis must fashion a democracy for themselves, no matter how different from our own.

"*Some commentators argue that . . . [Iraq] will not opt for a full-fledged theocracy . . . but leaving the issue to be decided by unlimited majority rule could be America's most deadly mistake.*"

The United States Should Not Permit Iraqis to Elect an Islamic Regime

Robert Garmong

Following Saddam Hussein's ousting in 2003, many outside observers called for the creation of democracy in Iraq. In the viewpoint that follows, Robert Garmong questions whether democracy should be pursued in that country. He argues that democracy can be a form of tyranny by majority rule and raises the possibility that the Shiite Muslims that form a majority in Iraq may vote in an Islamic theocracy similar to the one that has ruled Iraq's neighbor, Iran, since 1979. Permitting the Iraqi majority to choose Islamic leaders may result in a worse threat to American interests than the Saddam Hussein regime, he concludes. Garmong is a writer for the Ayn Rand Institute in California.

As you read, consider the following questions:
1. Why did America's Founders reject democracy, according to Garmong?
2. What is one of the hallmarks of democracy that Garmong finds worrisome?
3. What was the essential evil of Saddam Hussein's regime, according to the author?

Robert Garmong, "Liberty, Not Democracy, in Iraq," *MediaLink*, May 18, 2003. Copyright © 2003 by Ayn Rand® Institute (ARI). Reproduced by permission.

The bromide, often quoted today [in the aftermath of the 2003 war in Iraq], that we have won the war but now we have to "win the peace," is meant to remind us that we have to turn from achieving our military goals to achieving our political goals in Iraq. But what if our political goals were such that accomplishing them would obliterate the meaning of our military victory? Such is the nature of the Bush administration's stated goal of bringing "democracy" to Iraq.

What Iraq needs is not democracy, but liberty.

A Dangerous Term

"Democracy" is the most dangerous term in the American political lexicon. It has become a vague, warm-and-fuzzy label used to evoke the whole American system of government. Yet when America's Founders overthrew tyranny in this country, they emphatically rejected the notion of replacing it with another form of tyranny. For this reason, they expressly rejected democracy.

"Democracy," they recognized, actually means unlimited majority rule. If two men on a desert island vote to cannibalize the third, that is democracy. So it was when citizens of Athens, history's first democracy, voted to execute Socrates. And so it was when the German public voted for the Nazi Party. Democracy is not a system of liberty, but a form of tyranny: the tyranny of the majority.

Our Founders called the American system a "republic": a representative government limited by a constitution that protects the rights of the individual. Although the citizens of a republic vote for their leaders, voting is just a means to the end of protecting liberty. No matter what the people may wish their government to do, the Constitution is clear: Congress may pass no law that violates the rights of the individual. Such restrictions are codified in the Bill of Rights, the wall that protects our liberty from the whims of the majority.

Yet the tyranny of the majority is precisely what the Bush administration is pledging to leave behind in Iraq. Speaking to a group of Iraqi exiles, President [George W.] Bush insisted that "America has no intention of imposing our form of government or culture" on Iraq. Administration officials have repeatedly stressed that the form of Iraq's new government is to be determined by the Iraqi people, with the only goal being that it is "democratic." Whatever the Iraqi majority demands, it will get.

The Islamic Threat

A hallmark of democracy is pressure-group warfare, as each group seeks to claim the status of a majority and exploit all the rest. Iraqis have already begun forming up into ethnic and religious groups, each struggling to displace other groups from its traditional territory, each demanding the right to a share of "the people's" oil money. And every day, Iranian-backed religious leaders—with support from Iraqi Shiites—are extending their power and influence, positioning themselves to control the new, "democratic" Iraq.

Democracy and Islam

The most intractable problem facing democratic reform in Iraq (or anywhere else in the Muslim world) is how to reconcile that founding principle of democracy—the separation of church and state—with Islamic law, which is predicated on the inseparable union of religious and political power. . . .

Typical is the comment of . . . [a] Shi'ite imam to Agence France Presse. "Our objective is to set up an Islamic state, because this is the supreme ambition of all Arab and Muslim countries. All Muslim countries would like to see their governments applying sharia (Islamic law)."

This doesn't bode well for democracy, fledgling or otherwise.

Diana West, *Washington Times*, April 18, 2003.

It is too soon to predict the details, but we can already see in outline what form of tyranny Iraq's Shiite majority might choose. Clerics have begun strident calls for an Islamic state, and in a grim reminder of what that means, art studios and theaters have received warnings from Shiite clerics that they are to be shut down and converted to religious schools.

Some commentators argue that the relatively secular Iraqi culture will not opt for a full-fledged theocracy like Iran's. Perhaps—but leaving the issue to be decided by unlimited majority rule could be America's most deadly mistake. Yet 62 percent of respondents to a recent ABC News poll said

America should support an Islamic fundamentalist state in Iraq, if it gains power by "democratic" vote.

Betraying the War Effort

Leaving such a democracy in Iraq would be a betrayal of every value we sought to gain in this war. The essential evil of Saddam's Baathist ideology was its collectivism, the view that the "Arab Nation" is supreme and that the rights and interests of the individual may be sacrificed in service to its dictates. It makes no difference, in principle, if this "collective will" is divined by the edicts of a dictator or by majority vote—so long as the rights of the individual may still be sacrificed.

Anything-goes democracy in Iraq could be an even greater threat to American interests than the regime we have spent so much blood and money to topple. It is vitally important that our leaders make clear that they are attempting to leave behind a system of liberty, not democracy, in Iraq. It would be obscene to spend American lives to establish such a profoundly anti-American idea as the tyranny of the majority.

Periodical Bibliography

The following articles have been selected to supplement the diverse views presented in this chapter.

Robert J. Barro — "A Democratic Iraq Isn't an Impossible Dream," *Business Week*, March 31, 2003.

David Brooks — "Building Democracy Out of What?" *Atlantic Monthly*, June 2003.

Thomas Carothers — "Messy Democracy," *Washington Post*, April 8, 2003.

Dexter Filkins and Neil Macfarquhar — "U.S. Officials Tell Iraqis to Assert More Authority," *New York Times*, August 21, 2003.

Reuel Marc Gerecht — "Why We Need a Democratic Iraq," *Weekly Standard*," March 24, 2003.

Jim Hoagland — "De-Baathification, Root and Branch," *Washington Post*, April 24, 2003.

Efraim Karsh — "Making Iraq Safe for Democracy," *Commentary*, April 2003.

Eli J. Lake — "Split Decision," *New Republic*, May 5, 2003.

Chappell Lawson — "How Best to Build Democracy—Laying a Foundation for the New Iraq," *Foreign Affairs*, July/August 2003.

Felicia R. Lee — "Constitutionally, a Risky Business," *New York Times*, May 31, 2003.

Edward N. Luttwak — "Democracy in Iraq? It's a Fairy Tale," *Los Angeles Times*, August 5, 2003.

Donald H. Rumsfeld — "Core Principles for a Free Iraq," *Wall Street Journal*, May 27, 2003.

Jalal Talabani and Massoud Barzani — "What Iraq Needs Now," *New York Times*, July 9, 2003.

Jay Tolson — "Writing a Nation," *U.S. News & World Report*, May 26, 2003.

Fareed Zakaria — "Beware the Puppet Masters: All Those Groups and Leaders Who Lived Through Saddam Hussein's Reign Cannot Be Pleased to See the Exiles Being Foisted Atop the Country," *Newsweek*, August 11, 2003.

CHAPTER 4

What Lies in the Future for Iraq?

Chapter Preface

The population of Iraq includes a diverse array of religious and ethnic groups, including Assyrian Christians, ethnic Turks, and Armenians. However, most analyses of Iraq's population begin and end with its three largest groups: Kurds, Sunni Arabs, and Shiite (or Shia) Arabs, who together account for more than 95 percent of Iraq's total population. Kurds are concentrated in northern Iraq, Sunni Arabs in the central region, and Shiites in the southern part. Iraq's history has long been marked by conflict between these peoples. The question of whether these three groups, concentrated in different places, can long coexist as part of one united nation has become increasingly important in the aftermath of Saddam Hussein's fall in 2003.

Sunni Arabs and Shiite Arabs share Arabic as a common language and ethnicity but are fundamentally divided by religion. The Islamic world has been divided into two main branches for more than thirteen hundred years. Sunni Islam is the predominant branch in the Middle East and Africa. While only constituting around 20 percent of Iraq's population, Sunni Arabs have dominated Iraq's political life for most of the nation's modern existence, including during the reign of Saddam Hussein.

Shiites, who constitute about 60 percent of Iraq's population, have traditionally been politically suppressed in Iraq by the Sunni Arab minority. Following the 1991 Persian Gulf War, many Shiites rose in revolt only to be crushed by Hussein's regime. The Shiite branch of Islam, while a minority in most of the Muslim world, forms a majority in both Iraq and its neighbor Iran, which has been ruled by an Islamic theocracy since 1979. Some observers have predicted that Iraq's Shiites may attempt to create a similar Islamic theocracy in Iraq. (Although Shiites in Iraq share religious beliefs with Iranians, their Arabic language and ethnicity sets them apart from Iran's Shiites, who speak Farsi [Persian] and have a different cultural history.)

Iraqi Kurds are the nation's largest ethnic minority group, constituting about 23 percent of Iraq's population. Kurds, who speak a language related to Persian, and who for the most part are Sunni Muslims, have a long history as a distinct people but have never had their own country. Iraq and its neighbors, Iran and Turkey, all share restive Kurdish minority populations, and these three countries have long opposed ceding territory to create an independent Kurdish state. Kurdish insurgents fought Saddam Hussein throughout most of his rule in Iraq and were victims of chemical attacks by Hussein in 1988. Like the Shiites in the south, Kurds in the north attempted to revolt against Hussein after the 1991 war. Although Hussein remained in power, the Kurds were able to control some territory and establish a measure of self-rule in parts of northern Iraq that were "no-fly" zones (territory that American and British planes patrolled). Kurdish forces also fought alongside Americans in the 2003 war. While most Kurdish leaders in Iraq have pledged support for a united and federated post-Saddam Iraq, some have raised the possibility that the time has come for a separate Kurdish country.

The fall of Saddam Hussein in 2003 left the United States with the challenge of occupying Iraq and creating a new government that will eventually assume power. However, while many in America and Iraq are calling for a democratic form of government, some observers believe that such a government would give the majority Shiite population power over Kurds and Sunnis—a development unacceptable to most people belonging to those groups. "A real challenge to any post-Saddam Iraq," argues journalist and author Sandra Mackey, "is to devise a political system that gives the Shia their political and economic rights as a majority, but yet, at the same time, protects the rights of the minority." This challenge is but one of many Iraq faces, as the following viewpoints illustrate.

| *"Iraqi society is highly conducive to democracy."*

Iraq's Prospects for Democracy Are Good

Rend Rahim Franke

Rend Rahim Franke is executive director of the Iraq Foundation, a nonprofit organization that works for democracy and human rights in Iraq. The following viewpoint is drawn from remarks that she delivered at a January 2003 forum about the future of Iraq after Saddam Hussein is removed (the Iraqi dictator was deposed a few months later by a U.S.-led military coalition). Franke contends that Iraqi opposition groups are united in their support of democracy and that Iraqi society contains many elements favorable to creating democracy, including an urbanized and highly educated populace. Franke concludes by calling for the United States to take an active role in nurturing Iraqi democracy.

As you read, consider the following questions:

1. What "canard" about democracy does Franke criticize as being racist?
2. What elements of Iraqi society and culture does the author consider to be conducive to democracy?
3. Why does Franke call for the United States to take an active role in helping Iraq create a democracy?

As the international community debates [in January 2003] a military intervention to disarm Saddam Hussein, a larger moral issue is missing from the discussion: The Iraqi people's yearning for freedom. For decades, a nation of 24 million people has been oppressed in a way that is unprecedented since Hitler and Stalin. As the world considers regime change in Iraq, it should recognize that it faces a remarkable opportunity to change the fate of the Iraqi people for the better. This also could have dramatic repercussions beyond Iraq.

Removing Saddam Hussein would liberate the Iraqi people's energy and talents so that they may be directed towards good, not evil. A free Iraq would have sufficient critical mass in terms of its culture, its people, and its resources to galvanize the Arab and Islamic world. A free Iraq would unleash new voices and new visions for the people of the Middle-East, opening perspectives of freedom that have long been quashed by their autocratic rulers. The project of establishing democracy in Iraq should therefore be considered not only in terms of the benefits it would bring the Iraqi people, but also in terms of its catalyzing effect in the rest of the region. Success in Iraq would disprove the canard that democracy is not a realistic proposition for Muslims or Arabs—a racist idea that deserves to be challenged.

We should not underestimate the potential for democracy in Iraq, but nor should we overestimate the ease with which it will establish itself in the wake of decades of totalitarian rule. The key question is, what can and should the international community do to help the Iraqi people achieve the freedom that they, like all people of the world, aspire to and deserve.

Iraqis Want Democracy

A good starting point is the unity of the Iraqi opposition on the goal of democracy. Much has been reported about how diverse, if not fractious, the opposition is. It includes Sunnis, Shia's, Kurds and Christians; Islamists, Secular Democrats and Communists. But what is most remarkable about this diverse umbrella is its unity of vocabulary: Every faction of the opposition speaks the language of democracy. There is a broad consensus that a post-Saddam Iraq should be representative, decentralized and federal, with civilian control of the military and respect for individual rights and ethnic diversity. There are still debates about the precise structure of this federal system, but what is key is the agreement that power in a future Iraq should be devolved. This is a radical idea in the Middle-East.

Iraqi society is highly conducive to democracy. It has long been an urban society. Indeed, one of the tragedies of Saddam's rule has been his campaign to de-urbanize the culture of Iraqi society, with a massive social experiment designed to revive tribalism. Even so, Iraq's foundation remains largely urban. Iraqi society is also highly educated: It has the highest number of engineers per capita in the world, higher even than India. Iraq has a rich tradition of arts, culture and literature. Historically, Iraq and Egypt have competed not only for political leadership but also for the intellectual leadership of the Arab world. In addition, unlike other Arab societies, Iraqis began extensive interactions with the West as early as the 1930s, and as a result Iraqis have a broader worldview that blends Western ideas with Arab identity. Because of the extraordinary repression they have endured, the Iraqi people have a great thirst for freedom. Their pursuit of democracy will not be driven by the abstract ideas of intellectuals; it will be rooted in a deep and emotional desire for freedom arising from the long years of tyranny.

The greatest social challenges to democratization will be transforming the institutions of the state. All power in Iraq is concentrated in the hands of a single individual, Saddam Hussein, and this has affected how government functions and officials behave. Their mental energies are geared exclusively towards remaining in step with the will of Saddam. They do not think or act independently. While the ideology of the Ba'th may be only skin deep within the bureaucracy of the state, it has nevertheless left its mark in conformity and fear of innovation.

The legal and institutional foundations of Iraq have been subverted by Saddam's regime. The Iraqi constitution includes exemplary language that enshrines individual liberties, but infamous Article 42 gives the Revolutionary Command Council (RCC) the power to promulgate any edict, even if it contravenes all the other articles of the constitution. Thus, in one fell swoop, the entire constitutional basis of government in Iraq is nullified by the whims of Saddam Hussein, as expressed through the RCC. Adding to his tyranny is the fact that there are secret laws alongside public laws. Lack of knowledge of these secret laws is no defense for those who break them. The whole legal foundation of Iraq will need to be overhauled.

America's Stake in Iraq's Success

There are still difficulties in Iraq, to be sure—crime, inflation, gas lines, unemployment. But the fact that such difficulties exist should come as no surprise: No nation that has made the transition from tyranny to a free society has been immune to the difficulties and challenges of taking that path—not even our own.

As Thomas Jefferson put it, "we are not to expect to be translated from despotism to liberty in a featherbed." It took time and patience, but eventually our Founders got it right—and we hope so will the people of Iraq—over time.

We have a stake in their success. For if Iraq—with its size, capabilities, and resources—is able to move to the path of representative democracy, the impact in the region and the world could be dramatic. Iraq could conceivably become a model—proof that a moderate Muslim state can succeed in the battle against extremism taking place in the Muslim world today.

We are committed to helping the Iraqi people get on that path to a free society. We do not have an American "template" we want to impose: Iraqis will figure out how to build a free nation in a manner that reflects their unique culture and traditions.

Donald H. Rumsfeld, *Wall Street Journal*, May 27, 2003.

To create a modern politics in Iraq, political parties will need to be created that have national appeal and cut across the boundaries of ethnicity and religion. It will be most important to create avenues for political participation at the local, grassroots level. One of the detrimental effects of Saddam's reign is the Iraqi people's loss of faith in their ability to influence their environment and effect change. Iraqis barely have control over the details of their daily lives; the idea that they can be involved in shaping their collective destiny is inconceivable under Saddam Hussein. We will need to target Iraqi individuals and teach them to organize and advocate for their interests in their local communities and at the national level.

United States Should Take an Active Role

If the United States does not take an active role in nurturing Iraqi democracy, there are many elements both outside and within Iraq who will do everything they can to make sure it fails. Middle-Eastern autocrats understand all too well the danger that a successful democracy in Iraq poses to the regional status quo. The world, and the United States especially, as leader of the free world, should not content itself with replacing Saddam Hussein with a new autocrat, a dictator-lite. The United States should be committed and vigilant in ensuring that the building blocks of democracy are established. The Iraqi people will do their part; the international community should give us its support. Anything less will be a great opportunity foregone to dramatically change the fate of millions of Iraqis, and sow the seeds for even greater changes across the Middle-East.

"It's hard not to be pessimistic about the chances of Iraq establishing a stable, democratic political system."

Iraq's Prospects for Democracy Are Poor

Patrick Basham

In the following viewpoint, written shortly after the toppling of the regime of Saddam Hussein in 2003, Patrick Basham gives a pessimistic assessment of the chances that Iraq will replace Saddam Hussein's dictatorship with a viable democratic government. He contends that Iraq is torn by numerous religious, ethnic, and tribal divisions, and that Iraqi society lacks the economic development and cultural values necessary to create democracy. The concepts of political freedom and responsibility are alien to most Iraqis, he asserts. Basham is a senior fellow in the Center for Representative Government at the Cato Institute, a think tank that promotes limited government.

As you read, consider the following questions:
1. What possible negative outcome of majority Shiite rule in Iraq does Basham argue must be prevented?
2. What does the author consider to be the basic building blocks of democracy?
3. How many different tribes exist in Iraq, according to Basham?

Patrick Basham, "Flying Blind on the Path to a Democratic Iraq," *Cato Daily Commentary*, May 4, 2003. Copyright © 2003 by the Cato Institute. Reproduced by permission.

Vivid demonstrations of Shiite religious fervor and undemocratic intent (in April 2003) caught our political leaders completely off guard. While Gen. Tommy Franks clearly did his homework before engaging Iraq in military combat, there are red faces throughout the Bush administration over the lack of preparation for the political challenge of a post-Saddam [Hussein] Iraq.

How did this happen? Ironically, the Bush administration accepted the anti-war argument that Iraq was too secular a country to foster a populist, religious-based antipathy to American interests. In reality, however, the notion of a secular Iraq requires considerable qualification. Iraq's outward appearance largely stemmed from the Hussein regime's preference for institutionalized thuggery over religious fanaticism.

The Baathist party that provided Saddam's political backbone was philosophically and operationally fascist, inspired more by mid-century European Nazism than by dreams of an Islamic afterlife. Saddam sprang from central Iraq's minority Muslim sect, the Sunnis, whose moderation is measured relative to Iraq's Muslim majority, the southern-based Shiites, a significant proportion of whom adhere to the faith promulgated by Iran's fundamentalist Islamic leadership.

Iraq's Complex Society

Does the strength of the Shiite Muslim community foreshadow trouble for a democratic Iraq? The explosion of Shiite sentiment vividly illustrates the complex, heterogeneous nature of Iraqi society. There exist centuries-old religious and ethnic hatreds, as well as intense, frequently violent, tribal and clan rivalries.

A balance of power must be achieved, for example, between those subscribing to different interpretations of the Muslim faith. Iraq's new political institutions must be designed to prevent the long suppressed but currently better organized, more motivated, and better financed Shiites from exacting revenge upon the Sunnis and ignoring the needs of the northern Kurds, Christians, and urban secularists.

It's hard not to be pessimistic about the chances of Iraq establishing a stable, democratic political system in the short-to-medium term. This pessimism stems from an appreciation of what causes democracy to flourish in a society. The long-term survival of democratic institutions requires a particular political culture that solidly supports democracy.

Building Blocks of Democracy

The building blocks of a modern democratic political culture aren't institutional (e.g., elections, parties, legislatures, and constitutions) in nature. Rather, they are found in apt economic conditions (e.g., rising living standards and a large, thriving middle class) and supportive cultural values (e.g., political trust, political participation, tolerance of minorities, and gender equality). In practice, economic development stimulates higher levels of democratic values in the political culture. As a person's values change, these changes affect that person's political behavior producing higher, more stable levels of democracy.

Asay. © 2003 by Creators Syndicate. Reprinted with permission.

Clearly, the economic and cultural conditions prevalent in Iraqi society fall far short of what is found in all established democracies. Like many of its Arab neighbors, Iraq has failed to come to terms with the modern world. More than

75 percent of Iraqis belong to one of 150 tribes and significant numbers subscribe to a traditional tribal culture that manifests itself in everything from unquestioning obedience to tribal sheiks to such anachronistic customs as polygamy.

This is a deeply paternalistic political culture in which political leaders are frequently portrayed as larger-than-life, heroic figures able to rescue the masses from danger or despair. In such an environment, ordinary people adopt a political passivity that acts as a brake on the development of ideas, such as personal responsibility and self-help, central to the development of economic and political liberalism.

Iraqi political culture is still characterized by "identity politics," i.e., the elevation of ethno-religious solidarity over all other values, including individual liberty. Hence, political freedom is an alien concept to most Iraqis. The United States is attempting to sow the seeds of 21st century political institutions in the soil of a 15th century political culture. In coming seasons, a bountiful democratic harvest is an unrealistic prospect.

| *"Only a creative federalist political system tailored to the Iraqi people's needs will succeed."*

Iraq Needs a Federalist System of Government

Alon Ben-Meir

Alon Ben-Meir is a professor of international relations and Middle Eastern studies at New York University and a prolific writer and lecturer on the Middle East. In the following viewpoint he argues for a federalist political system in which Iraq's three main factions (Kurds, Shiites, and Sunnis) retain a significant measure of autonomy and self-rule through the creation of three separate states within Iraq. He argues that such a system, which borrows elements from the governments of the United States and other democracies, will prevent one ethnic group from violating the rights of the others and would create the conditions conducive for making Iraq a stable democracy.

As you read, consider the following questions:
1. What are some of the social and historical factors that make governing Iraq difficult, according to Ben-Meir?
2. How many years might it take to establish a working government in Iraq, according to the author?
3. What kind of political structures does Ben-Meir propose for Iraq's national government?

Alon Ben-Meir, "Democratizing Iraq," United Press International, April 27, 2003. Copyright © 2003 by United Press International. Reproduced by permission.

O *nly a creative federalist political system tailored to the Iraqi* *people's needs will succeed.*

Democratizing Iraq may prove to be a nightmare unless we build on the nation's inherent factionalism by developing a democratic political system that fully reflects Iraqis' communal, social, and "religious" diversity. Only through some form of federalism, whereby Iraq's three main factions—the Kurds, the Shiites, and the Sunnis—enjoy equal constitutional protection while exercising self-rule, will the country become a stable democracy.

The difficulties in governing Iraq stem from a number of factors—historical, psychological, religious, and communal. The disposition of its natural resources, including oil, also will come into play. These factors will doom any American plans to democratize Iraq based purely on our political philosophy of majority rule. The Iraqi people have gone through so many trials and tribulations. Only a political system that can respond to the needs bred out of these circumstances can endure. The country has never experienced anything resembling western democracy. For 400 years from 1515 to 1915, Iraq was part of the Ottoman Empire, then between 1920–1932, Britain controlled it. In 1958 the military overthrew the monarchy, and a few years later, in 1963, the Ba'ath socialist party took power. The decades of the 1960s and the 1970s were marked by one military coup after another. For one brief period, between 1922 and 1958, under the monarchy, the Iraqi people were given some semblance of freedom. A parliament was elected, and some legislators were allowed to debate and even to argue (with reverence) against the government without retribution. The press had limited freedom, as did the judiciary, although the powers they possessed not arbitrarily, favoritism was common. If the forms of government changed throughout much of the last 500 years, what did remain constant in Iraqi society was factionalism, tribalism, authoritarianism, and ethnic and sectarian violence. Loyalty was owed first to the head of the family, then to the head of the clan, and only then to the head of the tribe. Fidelity to the central authority always came last.

Most recently, the twenty-five years of ruthless rule by Saddam *Hussein have left most Iraqis embittered, disillusioned, cynical, suspicious, and impatient.* In the north are the Kurds who, having enjoyed under our protection autonomous rule for the past 12 years, are vehement about holding onto their gains and freedom, whatever party or sect becomes the central authority. In the center of the country, the dominant group, the Sunnis, have held the reins of power throughout Iraq's independence. They are not about to relinquish it to a democratically elected government unless they can ensure keeping some control. Mostly in the south are the Shiites, who have been deprived of power, even though they constitute about 60 percent of the population. They are hungry to assume the governance of their country. Given the choice, the Shiites, who are already actively jockeying for power, are the only group that would welcome direct elections, as these would certainly ensure their absolute dominance in any future government. But the United States wants to prevent the rise of Shiites, especially since all their leaders, including Ayatollah Ali al-Sestani, the country's most senior Shiite cleric, have made no secret of their determination to establish an Islamic republic in Iraq. Adding fuel to the fire of sectarian and political rivalries is the disposition of Iraq's natural resources, chiefly oil. These resources are not only a source of wealth but of contention and intense dispute. How the revenue generated from the riches of the land is shared and who will control them are serious problems that have created deep animosity in the past between the central government and the provinces.

A Federal System

If the objective of the Bush administration is to establish lasting democracy in Iraq, it must understand that the only viable option is to create a federal system. Such a system would have to ensure the representation of all Iraqis, guarantee human rights, liberty, political freedom, stability, and the equitable distribution of national wealth. We must develop such a system in four stages:

First, as we try to assemble a transitional Iraqi government, we must restore internal security, provide basic services, and begin to educate the leadership drawn from all backgrounds and communal persuasions—to think in terms of federalism.

How James Madison's Ideas on Federalism Apply to Iraq

Consider the remarks of James Madison in the *Federalist Papers*. In *Federalist 10*, Madison claims that the most important advantage of a well constructed Union is "its tendency to break and control the violence of faction." What he had in mind by the "violence of faction" is the tendency of one group, united by shared interests, to do violence to other groups that threaten its interests.

If one faction has the ability to gain control of a society—as the Ba'ath party did in Iraq—it is likely to abuse its power to pursue its own interests. But if many different factions, in shifting coalitions, are competing for power, Madison reasoned, then no one faction will be able to abuse power. Moreover, members of all factions will learn to respect the value of checks on power because, from time to time, at least in certain regards, all will be members of factions that are out of power.

Establishing a federal government in Iraq should give rise to such a system, one with many different factions in shifting coalitions. Each new, or newly empowered, province will form a faction of its own. If power is held largely at the national level, then each will compete for power on the national stage, rather than look to secede. If there are many provinces, and none is distinctly more powerful than the rest, then each will have to form coalitions with each other to have access to power. . . .

In addition, if the provinces do not line up neatly with the ethnic and tribal factions that already exist, then individuals will develop competing loyalties. Shiites, for example, may develop overlapping interests with Sunnis in their province, interests that would temper any interest the one group might have in pursuing a religious agenda that the others would consider oppressive.

Alec Walen, *FindLaw's Writ*, April 10, 2003.

We have to understand that such a political system will not readily resonate with the Shiites or the Sunnis for different reasons. The Shiites will have problems understanding the concept of shared powers because they believe their sheer numbers guarantee them control. For their part the Sunnis would like to assume that because they've always had the power, there is no reason for this not to continue. Despite these difficulties, as an all-Iraqi transitional government is established and begins to function under the direction and advice of the American civilian authority, the principles of federalism must guide all of our plans and actions. Such a government might need two years to establish.

Second, since no democratic form of government can be created in a vacuum, the transitional government must initially build the democratic institutions necessary to sustain social freedom and personal security. To that end, the first task of the government should be to write a constitution with a federal system as its core. The rights of the Iraqi people must be institutionally enshrined and supersede the power of any elected official. Concurrently, the government must begin in earnest to lay the foundations for a fair and impartial judiciary, free press, market economy, religious tolerance, freedom of expression and assembly, freedom of education, and the formation of political parties.

Three States

Third, the country should be divided into three major federal states: a northern state, with a majority of Kurds; a central state, with a majority of Sunni Muslims; and a southern state, with a majority of Shiites. Each state should have a number of provinces that are governed on the same basis as the state. The states will be empowered to run their own internal affairs as they see fit and to assume full control of their territories, except in matters involving natural resources. The states must also abide by federal laws. Each state should be equally represented in the Higher House (Senate) and proportionately in the Lower House (House of Representatives). A president serving a term of four years, and with only ceremonial responsibilities, should be chosen by the Lower House, and a prime minister, also serving a four-year term, but exercising full executive responsibilities, should be chosen by the Higher House. This type of arrangement will (1) provide equitable representation for all three major groups (2) prevent the president from assuming powers beyond the limits imposed by the constitution, and (3) give each of the three factions an equal opportunity to choose a prime minister based on merit, including his or her executive and administrative abilities.

Fourth, the federal authority must equally represent all three segments of the population, as well as minorities such as the Turkmen. The central authority will have several critical functions: (1) it will be in charge of external security and foreign affairs; (2) it will arbitrate disputes among the three federated states via a strong and impartial federal judiciary; (3) it will be in charge of a central Iraqi bank, which should regulate currency, maintain financial stability (including establishing a federal reserve), and redistribute funds from the sale of Iraqi oil proportionately and equitably to the regions; and (4) it will develop, and maintain, Iraq's strategic assets, such as oil, to ensure that all Iraqis benefit from their national wealth.

This type of political system borrows from a variety of systems including our own, Israel's, England's, Japan's and others. *To work, this system must satisfy the conflicting demands of the various rival groups.* Therefore, self-rule for the states, a strong central/federal government, and a system of checks and balances are fundamental to dealing with the sensibilities of the Iraqis. Such governing principles will lead to the eventual success of a full-fledged democratic Iraqi government.

VIEWPOINT

"Our ... goal should ... be ... promoting human freedom and security—whether that means one Iraq, or several."

Iraq May Need to Divide into Separate Countries

Ralph Peters

Iraq was created after World War I out of three provinces of the Turkish Ottoman Empire. In the following viewpoint, written shortly after the removal of Iraqi dictator Saddam Hussein in 2003, Ralph Peters argues that it may be impossible for Iraq to remain a single, unified state because of divisions between its main ethnic groups. Iraq's Shiites and Kurds, who have suffered under the rule of Iraq's Sunni Arabs, may long for their own nations, he argues, regardless of practical difficulties. While the United States should continue to aim for a democratic and unified Iraq, it should not stand in the way of Iraq's dissolution if that is what its people want, he concludes. Peters, a retired military officer, is a columnist and author of *Beyond Terror: Strategy in a Changing World.*

As you read, consider the following questions:
1. Does Peters believe that the United States should encourage secession by Iraq's Shiites or Kurds?
2. Why do rational arguments often fail to convince people not to create new nations, according to the author?
3. What have the Kurds done to deserve American respect, according to Peters?

Ralph Peters, "Must Iraq Stay Whole?" *Washington Post*, April 20, 2003. Copyright © 2003 by Washington Post Book World Service/Washington Post Writers Group. Reproduced by permission of the author.

Traditional wisdom insists that Iraq must remain in one piece. Washington subscribes to that belief. The Bush administration insists it will not permit the breakup of Iraq.

But what if some Iraqis prefer to live apart from others who slaughtered their families?

Certainly, our efforts to rehabilitate the region would go more smoothly were Iraq to remain happily whole within its present borders. Our initial efforts should aim at facilitating cooperation between and the protection of Iraq's ethnic and religious groups. But we also need to think ahead and to think creatively if we are to avoid being blindsided by forces we cannot control.

The Lesson of Yugoslavia

What if, despite our earnest advice, the people of Iraq resist the argument that they would be better off economically and more secure were they to remain in a single unified state? What if the model for Iraq's future were Yugoslavia[1] after the Cold War, not Japan or Germany after World War II?

The key lesson of Yugoslavia was that no amount of diplomatic pressure, bribes in aid or peacekeeping forces can vanquish the desire of the oppressed to reclaim their independence and identity. Attempts to force such groups to continue to play together like nice children simply prolong the conflict and intensify the bloodshed.

We are far too quick to follow Europe's example and resist the popular will we should be supporting. If the United States does not stand for self-determination, who shall?

This is not an argument for provoking secession by Iraq's Kurds or Shiites. Objectively viewed, Iraq's advantages as an integral state are indeed enormous, while the practical obstacles faced by any emerging mini-states would range from the problems of a landlocked Kurdistan in the north to the threat of religious tyranny in the Shiite south.

But reason does not often prevail in the affairs of states and nations. Passion rules. Kosovo, Macedonia and Bosnia[2]

---

1. Yugoslavia, a federation of six republics and two provinces, broke apart during the 1990s. The breakup was accompanied by war and ethnic violence.   2. former provinces or republics of the former Yugoslavia

remain dependent on foreign donations, black-marketeering and debt for their survival. Two of the three were born anew in blood, and all are troubled. But none of this matters to those who could not bear the arbitrary borders imposed on them by diplomats whose concerns did not include the popular will.

We live in an age of breakdown, of the dissolution of artificial states whose borders were imposed arbitrarily in the wake of the [1919] Versailles conference that concluded the Great War with peerless ineptitude. The world has suffered for nearly a century for the follies and greed of the European diplomats who redrew the world to suit their foreign ministries.

Unthinkingly accepting this legacy, we Americans assume we might convince one people after another that they cannot constitute a viable state on their own, that they must see reason. We might as well try to talk a friend out of a foolish love affair. Entire peoples, like individuals, must learn the hard way.

After the collapse of these rotting states, many a newly liberated population will indeed find that it cannot thrive on its own. Then these populations will begin building new, larger entities. But we cannot short-circuit the system of change and force them to see reason before they have tried the course of passion. Human beings are not made that way.

As we try to help the Iraqis rebuild their state, we should spare no reasonable effort to demonstrate to all parties concerned the advantages of remaining together. But we must stop short of bullying them—and well short of folly.

Even as we aim for a democratic, rule-of-law Iraq, we must consider alternatives if we are to avoid being bushwhacked by the guerrilla forces of history.

Suffering Under Sunni Arab Rule

Iraq's Kurds, Shiites and numerous minorities long have suffered under the rule of Sunni Arabs from the country's middle. We have witnessed widely varied reactions to the arrival of U.S. troops in Iraq (in 2003). Kurds welcomed us with flowers. Some Shiites cheered and applauded, but others—influenced by Iran—have been far more reticent, even hostile. The Sunni Arabs in the nation's heartland were Saddam Hussein's most enthusiastic supporters, although many also suffered under the old regime.

Federalism Is Not Possible in Iraq

Iraq is not and has never been a nation state. Under Saddam [Hussein], it has evolved into an extremely repressive regime in which power and privilege are concentrated in a single clan and its hangers-on; but it remains a multinational state, in some ways not unlike the former Yugoslavia. "The Iraqi people" does not exist. The country comprises several distinct ethnic and religious groupings, which have been at one another's throats for many years. Along with some elements in the fractious Iraqi opposition, the Americans talk of a federal Iraq in which these groups will live peacefully together. But history shows that such constructions are extremely fragile. Democracy—above all the federal variety—requires trust, but trust is a commodity in desperately short supply in communities divided by historical memories of savage conflict.

As events in the Balkans have shown, when an authoritarian multinational state collapses, the result is not federalism. It is war and ethnic cleansing.

John Gray, *New Statesman*, March 31, 2003.

All the peoples of Iraq need to adjust to a new reality. But Washington may need to adjust to new realities of its own. Having caused so much change, we dare not insist categorically that nothing else may change.

Above all, we should champion the Kurds, who have earned the world's respect. A long-suffering people divided by cruel borders,[3] they seemed to pose an insoluble dilemma, given the strategic dictates of realpolitik. The United States needed bases in Turkey, and Ankara would not countenance a Kurdish state. Turks, Arabs and Iranians all insisted the Kurds must remain divided, poor and powerless.

Now Turkey has betrayed us, while the Kurds fought beside us.[4] In a decade of de facto autonomy in Iraq's north, the

---

3. Most Kurds live in Iraq, Iran, or Turkey; all three countries have staunchly opposed an independent Kurdish nation. 4. The Turkish government refused to let American troops use Turkey as a staging ground for a northern invasion of Iraq in the 2003 war. Kurdish forces fought alongside American forces in northern Iraq in the same conflict.

Kurds proved they can run a civil, rule-of-law state. Cynics point out that a "free Kurdistan," surrounded by enemies, would lack access to the sea. But the Kurds would have oil, and oil can buy access. . . .

America Is a Positive Force for Change

The situation in Iraq is far more complex than any commentary can describe. But a few things are clear. The United States throughout its history has been the world's most positive force for change. Now we must prepare ourselves to help shape further changes we cannot prevent. We must concentrate on building a better future, not on defending Europe's indecent legacies.

At the end of the Iraqi experiment, our most important goal should not be preserving the relics of Versailles but promoting human freedom and security—whether that means one Iraq, or several.

"The country's oil riches can play a very important part in creating the foundations for economic development."

Iraq's Oil Resources Can Lay the Foundations for Future Development

Daniel Yergin

Iraq has one of the world's largest proven oil reserves. In the viewpoint that follows, historian and author Daniel Yergin examines how Iraq's petroleum resources can help create a foundation for economic and political development following years of misrule under Saddam Hussein. Iraq's oil industry cannot by itself rescue Iraq, he writes, especially if it is not managed properly. But Iraq's oil resources and the earnings they can generate give the country a crucial advantage in its attempt to transition to a market economy and a democratic system of government. Yergin, chairman of Cambridge Energy Research Associates, is the author of *The Prize: The Epic Quest for Oil, Money, and Power*, for which he received the Pulitzer Prize. He is also the author of *Commanding Heights: The Battle for the World Economy*, now a six-hour PBS series and on video and DVD.

As you read, consider the following questions:

1. What is the new *Gilgamesh* myth about Iraq's oil, according to Yergin?
2. How much money does the author say Iraq will need for its reconstruction?
3. What is the state of Iraq's oil industry and facilities, according to Yergin?

Daniel Yergin, "Oil Shortage," *Boston Globe Magazine*, May 25, 2003. Copyright © 2003 by the Globe Newspaper Company. Reproduced by permission of the author.

The epic *Gilgamesh* tells the story of a Noah-like flood that engulfs ancient Mesopotamia in what is now Iraq. A modern version of the *Gilgamesh* myth is around today. It is the story of how a great flood of oil will flow from the fields of Iraq, not only transforming the world oil market but also liberating Iraq from the economic desperation left behind by Saddam Hussein.[1]

Like so many myths, this modern *Gilgamesh* is partly true but also contains a great deal of exaggeration. Iraq is certainly a country with huge petroleum reserves. . . . But reserves in the ground and the ability to produce are different things. In recent years, Iraq has pumped less than 3 percent of the world's oil supplies. As an oil producer, Iraq has been in the upper second tier, behind such countries as Mexico, Venezuela, and Norway, about even with Britain, and somewhat ahead of Nigeria.

Huge Problems

But where it has few challengers is in the scale of its problems. The contrast between Hussein's pleasure palaces and the penurious condition of the country is stark. Thirty-five years under his domination took a country that had the potential, with its wealth and educated middle class, to join the ranks of the developed world and instead impoverished it and its people. Its gross domestic product on the eve of the war is only a quarter of what it was 25 years ago. As such, it is back to where it was in the 1940s, before the oil boom began.

Iraq desperately needs billions of dollars for basic health and education and to feed its people. Inflation is rampant. The costs of reconstruction—roads, phone systems, water supplies, electricity—are estimated on the order of $100 billion. Its international debt burden—borrowing, plus reparations resulting from its 1990 invasion of Kuwait—is at least $350 billion. Iraqi agriculture, which once exported wheat to Europe, is in bad shape. In recent years, 90 percent of the population has depended on the United Nations for food.

So thorough is the collapse that there is some question as

1. Hussein, who became president of Iraq in 1979, was deposed in April 2003 by a U.S.-led military coalition.

to whether Iraq really even has something that can properly be called an economy. There is no banking system. For the time being, there is not even a national currency.

All this adds to the quandaries facing the new Iraqi authorities. . . . How can political stability and, eventually, a democratic system be secured without a solid economic foundation? But how can there be a solid economic foundation without security and political stability?

In such circumstances, of course, it is a blessing to have oil. Unlike Afghanistan, Iraq can earn a living in the world economy from its oil exports—$17 billion to $20 billion a year. That's a lot of money. And no longer will a good part of it be siphoned off for Hussein's military machine, extraordinary lifestyle, and overseas bank accounts. Such revenues can make a significant contribution to the restoration of economic life in Iraq.

But, when measured against the requirements, these revenues from oil can be no more than part of the solution. To think anything more is to risk falling prey to the new *Gilgamesh* myth. . . .

A Transition Economy

There is, however imperfect, a useful analogy. It comes from the framework developed in *Commanding Heights: The Battle for the World Economy*, the book I wrote with Joseph Stanislaw. This is the story of how Asia went from being the poorest continent in the world four decades ago to being at the forefront of economic dynamism, how international trade and globalization turned into engines of world economic growth—and how what was once the communist world rejoined the market system.

That last point is of particular relevance. Look at the countries that Iraq modeled itself upon—the communist nations of Eastern Europe. Saddam Hussein's ruling Ba'ath Party was influenced first, during World War II, by Nazi ideology and then, after the war, by communism. And, though it is not well recognized, the communist model was where Iraq got its economic system. The whole program was lifted straight out of the Eastern European cookbook—central planning, extensive state ownership, grinding regulation of most everything. In the 1960s, in good Stalinist and Maoist imitation, it even collectivized its agriculture, which turned out to be a total disaster.

In the 1990s, after the fall of communism, countries like Poland, the Czech Republic, and Russia became known as "transition economies"—nations that were shifting, with no shortage of turbulence and uncertainty, from centrally planned communist systems to capitalist systems. They instituted private property; they sold off state companies; and they opened up to the rest of the world.

Seen this way and given its legacy, Iraq is the latest of the transition economies. And that's the way it looks to some of those who led their countries through the transition. Leszek Balcerowicz, currently head of Poland's central bank and the architect of Poland's post-communist reforms, recently observed, "Iraq's present condition is no more difficult than that of the central European countries 12 years ago."

Iraq's Assets

As a transition economy, Iraq has several potential sources of strength. It has a well-educated, technologically adept population. Long before the Ba'ath Party took over, Iraq had strong trading and entrepreneurial traditions, and those have survived. China's stunning economic growth has benefited enormously from the "overseas Chinese" in Taiwan, Singapore, and elsewhere who have come back to their ancestral homes with capital, technology, and links to the world economy. Iraq could similarly benefit from the "overseas" Iraqis—equivalent to almost 20 percent of the population. These are not the Iraqis who would vie for political leadership but the ones who would go into business, often through their family links, bringing with them skills, capital, and connections to the world economy. There is a giant appetite for investment and a huge pent-up demand for goods and services. . . .

Every one of these potential assets, of course, can be qualified. For instance, in recent years, the educational system has broken down. The entrepreneurial traditions have survived mainly in the black market. Overseas Iraqis have to feel safe if they are to consider returning. As the Russians found in the 1990s, to move from a "bazaar" to a market economy requires the establishment of the rule of law and the sanctity of contract, which does not happen overnight. Poland's transition benefited enormously from the establishment of something like 2 million small businesses. To prime that kind of entrepreneurial energy in Iraq will require things that do not currently exist, such as a banking system and access to credit. And it is very hard to see how any of this can really happen without a modicum of security and political stability.

Iraq's Oil Challenges

With all that said, Iraq goes into the transition with something that most East European countries did not have—oil. But petroleum is not an unalloyed blessing. If not managed right, it can distort the economy, stunting the non-oil private sector and promoting corruption.

Will a new Iraq be able to use its oil as part of the larger process of reconstruction in such a way as to make the nation into something more than an oil state? That will be no small test.

That big flood of new oil is still well in the future. The challenge today for the Iraqi oil industry is clear—to fix itself. Since Saddam Hussein's fateful decision to invade Iran in 1980, the industry has been in continuing decline. In 1990, on the eve of the Kuwait invasion, the maximum Iraq could manage to produce was 3.5 million barrels per day. Since then, its capacity has fallen by about 20 percent—to 2.7 million barrels per day.

The industry is in a state of dilapidation. The underground reservoirs, from which the oil is pumped, have been damaged by years of mismanagement. The entire infrastructure—whether wells, pipelines, pumping stations, or ports—is in poor shape. Equipment is rusting and malfunctioning. Environmental pollution is widespread. That the whole apparatus is able to operate even at current levels is testament to the skill of Iraqi engineers. They have been geniuses at improvisation.

But ingenuity won't do the job alone. "The first task for the oil authorities," former Iraqi oil minister Issam Chalabi

says, "is to get production capacity back into proper shape."
For openers, that means coming up with $5 billion or more
to repair and upgrade infrastructure. It could take two or
even three years just to get the oil industry back to where it
was in 1990.

Iraq's Oil Production and Consumption, 1980–2002

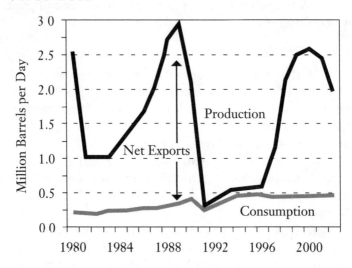

Note: Production includes crude oil, lease condensate, natural gas liquids, ethanol, and refinery gain.

Energy Information Administration, 2003.

Some of that time will be spent getting organized. There
is a shortage of talent. "Many highly skilled personnel have
left the country," says Chalabi, creating what he calls "one
generation gap or even two." Making recovery in the oil
fields more difficult is the extensive postwar looting and lack
of security. . . .

It is hard to find a sentence written anywhere that men-
tions Iraq's proven oil reserves without including something
like "second largest in the world, after Saudi Arabia." That
used to be true. But no longer. Iraq by some measures has
been overtaken by Canada.

The figure used for Iraqi reserves is 112 billion barrels,

which compares with 262 billion barrels for Saudi Arabia—and 22 billion for the United States. But bear in mind that this number came from a government not exactly known for its credibility. In the 1970s, Hussein had forbidden disclosure of any oil data, with dire consequences for not obeying. Subsequently, Iraq's proven reserves were listed at 65 billion barrels. Then, in the mid-1980s, at a time when other Organization of Petroleum Exporting Countries were increasing their proven reserves with a stroke of the pen, Iraq raised its number to more than 100 billion barrels.

Whatever the figures, Iraq has tremendous potential, owing to some huge underexplored and undeveloped oil fields. Perhaps a decade from now, Iraq's reserves will turn out to be much larger than the current numbers suggest. But, as with everything else involving Iraqi oil, it will take time and money to tap into them.

Here is where we come to the modern *Gilgamesh* myth—the notion that vast amounts of additional oil will soon flood from Iraq. In reality, major oil development requires big spending and is governed by what might be called "the law of long lead times." People talk ambitiously about Iraq's adding another 2 million barrels per day within three to four years. That's a great deal of oil—the equivalent of creating another Kuwait. But it's not cheap. The cost of adding another 2 million barrels per day of production capacity is estimated at $30 billion-plus. And it probably will take seven to 10 years to get there. . . .

A New Beginning

It has become common these days, when looking at the troubles of countries as different as Nigeria and Venezuela, to talk about the "curse of oil." And it would be hard to say that Iraq has not suffered from an oil curse. After all, with all the benefits oil has brought to Iraq, it has also enabled Saddam Hussein to lead the nation into disaster and its people into poverty.

But now, Iraq is at a new beginning. And petroleum can again be an enabler, depending on how the resources are managed and integrated into Iraq's larger prospects. The country's oil riches can play a very important part in creating the foundations for economic development and a new middle class and for the emergence of democracy. They also provide enormous temptation for corruption and diversion and for squandering of opportunity. Iraq has been there before.

"Oil is the only major source of revenues for Iraq, as it has been for well over 50 years," says Chalabi, the former oil minister. "But that does not mean that Iraq should depend upon oil for the next 50 years. We need to diversify our economy. We need to find other means of generating income. We need a growing private sector. We need foreign trade. We need foreign investment. But, in the meantime, we need oil to get there."

"American postwar planners are naive in thinking that oil will facilitate democracy in Iraq."

Iraq's Oil Resources May Hinder Future Development

John B. Judis

Some analysts have suggested that Iraq's significant oil wealth will help it make the transition from dictatorship to democracy following the fall of longtime dictator Saddam Hussein in April 2003. In the following viewpoint John B. Judis argues that Iraq's oil wealth, far from being an advantage, may actually be a hindrance to fashioning a viable democracy. He contends that oil wealth tends to strengthen authoritarian regimes that no longer have to rely on tax revenue. Oil wealth also retards the development of civil society—institutions such as social clubs, private businesses, and unions that exist independent of the state and which are, according to Judis, vital to creating a democratic form of government. Judis, a senior editor at the *New Republic*, has also written for the *American Prospect*, *Foreign Affairs*, and *Dissent*.

As you read, consider the following questions:

1. What made Norway the exception to most oil states, according to Judis?
2. Why has oil wealth not resulted in the creation of an independent business class in oil states?
3. What are some of the ways Saddam Hussein has spent Iraq's oil revenues?

John B. Judis, "Blood for Oil: Will Black Gold Stymie Democracy in Iraq?" *New Republic*, March 31, 2003, p. 20. Copyright © 2003 by The New Republic, Inc. Reproduced by permission.

A sk pessimists why Iraq will never be a democracy, and they most often cite its ethnic and religious divisions. A post–Saddam Hussein Iraq, they warn, could devolve into an Arab Yugoslavia,[1] with open warfare between the Sunnis, Shia, and Kurds, and with Iran, Turkey, and Saudi Arabia taking sides. Optimists . . . respond that a federation could manage these divisions. Except that federations don't work well in countries where mineral wealth is concentrated in potentially secessionist regions, as the experiences of Nigeria, Sierra Leone, and the former Belgian Congo attest. And most of Iraq's oil lies away from Baghdad, near the Kurdish North and in the Shia South.

But there's another—potentially greater—obstacle to democracy that gets much less attention, perhaps because American policymakers mistakenly see it as an advantage rather than a serious problem. And that is oil itself. As Vice President Dick Cheney put it . . . , "This is not a nation without resources, and, when it comes time to rebuild and to make the kinds of investments that are going to be required to give them a shot at achieving a truly representative government, . . . Iraq starts with significant advantages." On its face, Cheney's statement simply echoes [political scientist] Seymour Martin Lipset's famous adage: "The more well-to-do a nation, the greater its chances to sustain democracy." But, according to political scientists and economic historians, oil states are the exception that prove Lipset's rule: Oil wealth actually hinders, rather than helps, a country's transition to democracy, *Newsweek* columnist Fareed Zakaria makes this argument in his important new book, *The Future of Freedom.* If he and the academics are correct, American postwar planners are naive in thinking that oil will facilitate democracy in Iraq. Rather, they will have to figure out how to avoid the authoritarian fate that has befallen almost every other nation that has become dependent on oil.

Democracy is based, above all, on the separation of civil society from the state. It depends on the existence of an independent realm of social and economic power, protected

---

1. a multiethnic European country that violently broke apart into separate nations in the 1990s

from arbitrary state power by the rule of law. The components of civil society include what [French writer Alexis de] Tocqueville called "civil and political associations"—social clubs, churches, charitable organizations, and political parties—but the most important are private businesses and unions organized in a competitive, capitalist marketplace. It is these institutions—not the formal apparatus of elections—that guarantee popular self-rule by erecting a barrier against lawless government. Without these underpinnings, individuals and groups are absorbed into the all-powerful state, as they were under communist and fascist rule, and still are under many of today's authoritarian regimes. Elections become merely staged rituals.

In the United States, democracy arose largely through the spread of entrepreneurial capitalism in the early nineteenth century, the product of the small farmers and urban craftsmen whom Thomas Jefferson and Andrew Jackson celebrated. In Great Britain, democracy grew out of the millennial struggles among the king, landed aristocracy, business, and, finally, labor. . . . The struggle for liberty, as Zakaria puts it, preceded democracy. In continental Europe, labor's rise spurred an initial move toward democracy, but it took World War II to sever the link between big business and the state and military that had made fascism possible. In countries such as South Korea and Taiwan today, independent labor, business, and professional organizations are allowing democracy to emerge tentatively from what were once command economies.

It is no coincidence that this transition has not happened in countries with massive oil wealth. Today, Norway is the only full-fledged democracy that depends primarily on oil for its export income. But Norway was already a democracy with an independent civil society when it found oil in the North Sea in the 1960s. The rest of the world's oil nations had authoritarian regimes before they struck black gold. Many of them, including Iraq, Kuwait, and Algeria, were colonial possessions. Some, such as Iraq and Libya, were arbitrarily created by their European conquerors out of separate provinces. Most either already had monarchical traditions of rule or had them imposed on tribal, patrimonial systems by their colonial overseers. The British, for instance, imposed a king on the newly created Iraq in 1921.

Oil Strengthens Authoritarian Regimes

Oil wealth didn't undermine these authoritarian structures; it strengthened them. After the colonial powers departed at the end of World War II, oil provided the newly independent governments of the Middle East a veritable windfall—either through concessions or later through outright ownership of their country's oil facilities. With their new income, the states' kings, emirs, and sheiks were no longer dependent on their countries' merchants or workers for tax income. They could finance their governments entirely out of oil revenues. They could also use these oil revenues to buy off the citizenry through social-welfare systems, state jobs, land grants, and lucrative contracts. Their citizens became passive recipients of government largesse—paying no taxes and receiving no representation. . . .

In the Middle East, oil wealth provided a shortcut around the centuries-old transition from feudalism to capitalism and from absolutism to democracy that had taken place in Western Europe. The oil states did not have to endure the privations of what Karl Marx called the "primitive accumulation of capital." They didn't have to coerce peasants to leave their land to become impoverished wage-laborers in order to provide profit margins for fledgling entrepreneurs. They didn't have to extract taxes from a reluctant population. And they didn't have to grant democratic rights to a citizenry that grew increasingly restive under these demands. Because of its oil wealth, Libya could go from one of the poorest countries in the world, with a per capita income of $50 in 1960, to one of the well-to-do, with a per capita income of $2000 just a decade later, without exacting sacrifice from its people. Lost in this developmental shortcut, however, was the creation of an active citizenry, a thriving civil society, and a democratic political system.

Today, all of the world's oil nations, except Norway, have either authoritarian governments, such as those in Saudi Arabia and Iraq, or what Carnegie Endowment for International Peace political scientist Marina Ottaway calls "semiauthoritarian" governments. Some of the latter, such as Algeria, Indonesia, and Nigeria, have embraced aspects of democracy only to fall back onto authoritarianism and one-party domination as oil revenues have provided the means for repression and corruption as well as co-optation.

One might assume that, as these oil nations grew wealthier and their surplus profits spilled over into the population and fueled new investments, they would eventually create an independent business class not directly dependent on the state or its oil revenues. That class would in turn provide the basis for an independent civil society and for democracy. That could still happen, but it has not so far, and the reason lies in the peculiar influence that oil wealth exerts.

Oil wealth has not inspired but rather stifled the development of an autonomous bourgeoisie. It has increased citizen incomes, but it has not led to economic growth outside the oil industry. In most oil-rich countries, agriculture and non-oil industries have shrunk or disappeared entirely. Iraq became a net food importer in the early '70s. . . .

"Dutch disease," after what happened to Dutch industry during the '60s with the discovery of North Sea oil. In oil states, oil revenues boost exports and therefore tend to increase a country's exchange rate. By 1982–1983, after a decade-long oil boom, exchange rates in seven oil countries were 40 percent higher than in 1970–1972. That made these countries' exports more expensive to purchase and therefore undermined any incentive for entrepreneurs to start non-oil industries. Oil wealth also boosts average wages for skilled workers, pricing many fledgling industries out of the world market.

Several Arab governments, facing declining oil revenues, have sought to develop more diversified and independent industries, but they have been constrained by the nature of the states they created. Oil states, which depend on free trade to ensure their export revenues, can't start using tariffs to protect fledgling manufacturing industries. And, when governments in the Gulf states and Libya, like governments in other underdeveloped countries, have tried to privatize government businesses, they have run into popular resistance and resistance from within their own ranks. [Political scientist F. Gregory] Gause writes of the Gulf states, "First and foremost, privatization means a loss of at least some measure of control over the economy. [These] regimes, having spent the last three decades consolidating their dominance of their economies, are reluctant to give that up. . . . [P]rivatization also means higher prices for consumers used to subsidized goods and services.". . .

Bush administration officials who think they can take the countries of the Middle East directly from oil autocracies to democracies are repeating historic mistakes. Vladimir Lenin and Leon Trotsky thought they could take Russia directly from peasant feudalism to proletarian socialism. Mao Zedong wanted to leap past socialism directly to communism. And Libya's Muammar Qaddafi imagined a stateless utopia on the desert sands. But the history of the Arab oil states shows the difficulty of building democracy in countries that have not yet developed full-fledged capitalist economies. When democratic reforms are introduced in a society that lacks a thriving civil society sustained by independent business- and working-class organizations, reform can create despotic reaction rather than freedom. In the Middle East, monarchy has given way to Libya's neo-communist tyranny and to Iran's theocracy.

Iraq and Oil

Iraq is not an exception to this sorry history of reform-turned-despotism. After World War I, the British assembled Iraq out of three Ottoman-controlled provinces and installed King Faisal on the throne. In 1958, a military coup toppled King Faisal II. The overthrow of the Hashemite monarchy led to a tyranny—a mix of Stalinism and tribal warlordism—in which, according to historian Charles Tripp, "exclusivity, communal mistrust, patronage, and the exemplary use of violence constitute the main elements." In 1968, Saddam's Baath Party seized power.

Oil played a leading role in this continuing drama. In fact, it has mixed with ethnic infighting to make despotism even nastier in Iraq than in its neighboring oil states. Oil was first discovered in 1927, but it was not until the mid-'50s that oil revenues, based on concessions from the Anglo-American

Iraqi Petroleum Company (IPC), furnished most of state revenues. The military, led by General Abd Al Karim Qasim, seized power in 1958 partly on the grounds that the monarchy was too subservient to British oil. The United States helped Saddam and the Baath Party temporarily seize power in 1963 because they feared Qasim would nationalize the IPC; but, in 1972, after the Baath Party and Saddam had regained power, they turned around and nationalized the IPC themselves, which contributed to a dramatic increase in oil revenues in the '70s.

The Curse of Oil Wealth

In Iraq, with food, water, medicine and electricity shortages still making a nightmare of everyday life, and no democratic elections on the horizon, there is little likelihood that Iraqis will design an oil-revenue management system that directly benefits the citizenry soon, experts say.

They point to cautionary lessons from around the world, where almost invariably oil wealth has proved to be a curse. . . .

Iraq could privatize its oil industry, but that could set off ethnic fighting among Shiites, Kurds and Turkmens who live in the oil-rich areas—or end up enriching a handful of corrupt Iraqis, just as a small group of "oligarchs" benefited from the break-up of the oil industry in the former Soviet Union.

Marego Athans, *Baltimore Sun*, June 2, 2003.

During the oil boom of the '70s, the Baath Party and Saddam (who consolidated his power in 1979) used their newfound oil wealth to establish patronage networks and buy off the populace with generous social welfare expenditures on health, education, food, and housing. Like other oil states, Iraq created an enormous government bureaucracy that swallowed any hint of independent civil society. From 1958 to 1977 to 1991 the number of Iraqis employed by the state ballooned from 20,000 to 580,000 to 822,000. And these figures don't include the armed forces and pensioners who received all their income from the state. By 1991, according to University of Amsterdam political scientist Isam Al Khafaji, about 40 percent of Iraqi households were directly dependent on the state for their livelihood. But Iraq also devoted almost half of its oil revenue to building an extensive army and police force to fight the Kurds—who in 1969 had attacked the Kirkuk oil fields—and neighboring Iran, which backed the regime's Shia and Kurd opponents.

Iraq's oil income began to decline in the '80s because of the drop in world prices. Iraq also faced huge expenditures from its eight-year war with Iran and later its attempt to annex Kuwait. The decline in Iraq's standard of living, along with the massive death toll exacted by two wars, inspired opposition to Saddam's rule. But, rather than coming from merchants, manufacturers, labor unions, or political parties—the building blocks of a future democracy—it came from dissident Shia networks, secessionist Kurds, and the military. Unlike Iran or the Gulf states, Iraq doesn't have a noticeable, potentially dissident intelligentsia inside the country. Much of its professional class fled during the '80s, and the regime's attempt to diversify Iraqi industry in the late '80s fell flat. On the eve of [the 2003] war, much of the opposition inside Iraq still appears to consist of the Kurds, whose demand for autonomy could fracture the regime, and the Shia, who take their leadership from conservative Islamic clerics. Saddam may also have his critics in the military and in the Sunni-dominated bureaucracy, but they are not the kind of people who are well-suited to lead a democratic transformation.

None of this suggests that the Bush administration, aided by returning Iraqi professionals and Ahmed Chalabi's Iraqi National Congress, could not begin to reconstitute an Iraqi state. But it will not likely be a democratic one. Given the political history of oil states, America's primary objective should not be to immediately hold nominal elections but to gradually create a social and economic infrastructure that can sustain elected governments over the coming decades.

In *The Future of Freedom*, Zakaria argues that fledgling democracies have been best off with liberal authoritarian regimes like those that initially ruled South Korea and Taiwan and still govern Singapore. These regimes established not only order but also the rule of law and the market. They created the underpinnings for the rise of stable democracy. But, while South Korea and Taiwan had to survive treacherous transitions to democracy, they had the odd benefit of having to fall back on their own entrepreneurs and citizenry for the creation of wealth. A new regime in Baghdad will not only have to overcome a fractious citizenry and potentially hostile neighbors but also what political scientists call the "resource curse." A post-Saddam Iraq will have to do what no other Middle Eastern or African oil state has yet succeeded in doing: building a viable, independent civil society on the economic foundation of black gold. If Cheney doesn't understand the difficulties of doing that now, he will soon.

Periodical Bibliography

The following articles have been selected to supplement the diverse views presented in this chapter.

Russell Berman et al.	"The Dilemma of Reforming a Post-Saddam Iraq," *Commentary*, May 2003.
Babak Dehghanpisheh and Christopher Dickey	"The Shiite Shockwave," *Newsweek*, May 5, 2003.
Economist	"The Hard Path to New Nationhood: Rebuilding Iraq," April 16, 2003.
Bay Fang	"Trading Places," *U.S. News & World Report*, April 28, 2003.
Reuel Marc Gerecht	"How to Mix Politics with Religion," *New York Times*, April 29, 2003.
Eliza Griswold	"With the Kurds," *Nation*, April 14, 2003.
Lawrence F. Kaplan	"Federal Reserve—The State Department's Anti-Democracy Plan for Iraq," *New Republic*, March 17, 2003.
Laura King	"After the War/Fearing the Future; Women Fear Their Rights Will End with Hussein Era," *Los Angeles Times*, April 27, 2003.
Marianne Lavelle	"Priming the Pump," *U.S. News & World Report*, April 21, 2003.
Josh Martin	"Rebuilding Iraq: What Role Will Arabs Play?" *Middle East*, June 2003.
Yitzhak Nakash	"The Shi'ites and the Future of Iraq," *Foreign Affairs*, July/August 2003.
Martin Peretz	"Minority Rule—Who Shouldn't Run Iraq," *New Republic*, April 21, 2003.
Michael Rubin	"Are Kurds a Pariah Minority?" *Social Research*, Spring 2003.
Megan K. Stack	"After the War; Shiites Push for Political Power in Iraq; Many of the Sect's Leaders Are Set on Creating an Islamic Government. Some Vow to Resist Any U.S.-Imposed Secular Rule," *Los Angeles Times*, April 29, 2003.
Zainab Al-Suwaij	"Iraq's Silenced Majority," *New York Times*, May 23, 2003.
Jay Tolson	"Writing a Nation," *U.S. News & World Report*, May 26, 2003.

Patrick E. Tyler	"Cheers and Grumbles for Democracy and a Would-Be King," *New York Times*, June 11, 2003.
Milton Viorst	"Iraq; Why They Don't Want Democracy," *Los Angeles Times*, May 25, 2003.
Kevin Whitelaw	"The New-Style Iraqi Politics," *U.S. News & World Report*, June 2, 2003.
Adam Zagorin	"Iraq's Debt Bomb," *Time*, April 21, 2003.

For Further Discussion

Chapter 1

1. George W. Bush argues that the "risks of inaction" in regard to Iraq's threat to national security could be great because in a few years Iraq could have greater military capabilities. He justifies war as a way to prevent the rise of a stronger Iraq. Do you agree that such a preventive war is just and necessary? Explain your answer.

2. Contrary to John E. Farley's warnings, the 2003 war on Iraq did not in fact result in "massive" casualties. Does the failure of this prediction to come true weaken the rest of his arguments? Why or why not?

3. George W. Vradenburg argues that war on Iraq can be justified solely on the grounds of ending the suffering of Iraq's people. Do you agree or disagree? Could such a position be used to justify war against any number of tyrants? Explain.

4. Michael Massing argues that any benefits resulting from the war against Iraq must be weighed against any costs that incur. What does he see as the main costs of an American war against Iraq? Do you believe the costs he describes outweigh the potential net benefit of war to Iraq's people? Explain why or why not.

5. David Corn presents an excerpt of an imagined speech that an "honest" President Bush should have delivered to the American people prior to war. What are the main differences between Corn's version and the speech Bush actually gave (which is the first viewpoint of this chapter)? Do you believe Corn is being fair or unfair in his treatment of Bush? Defend your answer.

6. After reading the arguments of Michael Schrage as well as the other viewpoints in this chapter, do you believe that a failure to find weapons of mass destruction in Iraq would fatally undermine the case for war in 2003? Defend your answer with examples and arguments from the viewpoints.

Chapter 2

1. Should the fact that Philip Carter is a former army officer lend greater credence to his arguments for higher U.S. troop levels in Iraq, in your opinion? Why or why not?

2. What kind of promises to Iraq does Vito Fossella make on behalf of the United States? Does he quantify or delineate America's commitments? Does Carter's article cast doubt in your mind about Fossella's pledges? Explain.

3. What are the main differences between Max Boot's and Awad Nasir's conceptions of the Iraqi people and their preparedness for self-government? What evidence and arguments does each present to support his position?

4. Max Boot argues that America should not be hindered by fears of being called "imperialist." But Awad Nasir argues that many Iraqis share a fear of being dominated by foreign powers and maintains that the United States must take this into account. Do Boot's and Nasir's positions necessarily contradict each other? Explain. If you do perceive a contradiction, which author do you find most persuasive? Defend your answer.

5. Which of the five reasons listed by Joseph R. Biden and Chuck Hagel for involving the United Nations in the postwar reconstruction of Iraq are the strongest, in your opinion? Which are the weakest? Can you think of other reasons why the United Nations should be more involved? Explain.

6. After reading the viewpoints of Biden/Hagel and Nile Gardiner, do you believe that only those nations that fought the 2003 war should play a role in the postwar administration of Iraq? Why or why not?

Chapter 3

1. Barham Salih presents himself as an Iraqi and draws on his experience governing Kurdish-controlled Iraq. Amir Butler identifies as a Muslim and draws on his religious beliefs. Considering their respective backgrounds, which author do you find most convincing? Explain.

2. Salih generally has positive things to say about the United States and its decision to invade Iraq, while Butler expresses some critical views on American intervention. Do their pro and anti-American stances affect how you respond to their arguments? Could and should attachments to one's own country affect a person's views on the issues raised by Salih and Butler? Defend your answer.

3. Both Daniel Pipes and Laith Kubba argue that Iraq needs a transitional period during which order is established before democracy can be created. What are their basic disagreements on how this transition could be accomplished? Explain, citing examples from the viewpoints.

4. Robert Garmong criticizes democracy as a "tyranny of the majority." Do you agree or disagree with his stance? After reading his arguments and those of Joan Ryan, do you believe that the United States has the right to prevent the majority of people in

Iraq from electing a theocratic Islamic government if that is what they want? Explain your answer.

Chapter 4

1. Rend Rahim Franke's arguments were delivered and published in the weeks just preceding the American-led 2003 war against Iraq. Is this context important in evaluating her arguments about Iraq's commitment to democracy? Explain why or why not.

2. The Cato Institute, where Patrick Basham works, opposed the 2003 war in Iraq because it did not believe America's national security is affected by whether Iraq is a democracy or not. How do Basham's arguments on Iraq's prospects for democracy dovetail with the position of his institution?

3. After reading the viewpoints by Alon Ben-Meir and Ralph Peters, place yourself in the position of a Kurd, Shiite, or Sunni Muslim in Iraq. Would you want to have your own country or be part of Iraq? Why? And, how might you persuade a person from a different group of your position?

4. After reading the viewpoints of John B. Judis and Daniel Yergin, do you believe Iraq's oil resources are a net positive or negative asset for the country? Defend your answer, using evidence and arguments from the viewpoints.

Organizations to Contact

The editors have compiled the following list of organizations concerned with the issues debated in this book. The descriptions are derived from materials provided by the organizations. All have publications or information available for interested readers. The list was compiled on the date of publication of the present volume; the information provided here may change. Be aware that many organizations take several weeks or longer to respond to inquiries, so allow as much time as possible.

American Enterprise Institute (AEI)
1150 Seventeenth St. NW, Washington, DC 20036
(202) 862-5800 • fax: (202) 862-7177
website: www.aei.org

The American Enterprise Institute for Public Policy Research is a scholarly research institute that is dedicated to preserving limited government, private enterprise, and a strong foreign policy and national defense. Its publications on Iraq include articles in its magazine *American Enterprise* and books including *Study of Revenge: The First World Trade Center Attack and Saddam Hussein's War Against America*. Articles, speeches, and seminar transcripts on Iraq are available on its website.

Arms Control Association (ACA)
1726 M St. NW, Washington, DC 20036
(202) 463-8270 • fax: (202) 463-8273
e-mail: aca@armscontrol.org • website: www.armscontrol.org

The ACA is a national membership organization that works to educate the public and promote effective arms control policies. It publishes the magazine *Arms Control Today*. Documents and articles on nuclear, chemical, and biological weapons in Iraq can be found on its website.

The Brookings Institution
1775 Massachusetts Ave. NW, Washington, DC 20036
(202) 797-6000 • fax: (202) 797-6004
e-mail: brookinfo@brook.edu • website: www.brookings.org

The institution, founded in 1927, is a think tank that conducts research and education in foreign policy, economics, government, and the social sciences. Its Saban Center for Middle East Policy develops programs to promote a better understanding of policy choices in the Middle East. Articles on Iraq can be found on the organization's website and in its publications including the quarterly *Brookings Review*.

Center for Strategic and International Studies (CSIS)
1800 K St. NW, Suite 400, Washington, DC 20006
(202) 887-0200 • fax: (202) 775-3199
website: www.csis.org

The center works to provide world leaders with strategic insights and policy options on current and emerging global issues. It publishes books including *The "Instant" Lessons of the Iraq War*, the *Washington Quarterly*, a journal on political, economic, and security issues, and other publications including reports that can be downloaded from its website.

Education for Peace in Iraq Center (EPIC)
1101 Pennsylvania Ave. SE, Washington, DC 20003
(202) 543-6176
e-mail: info@epic-usa.org • website: http://epic-usa.org

The organization works to improve humanitarian conditions in Iraq and protect the human rights of Iraq's people. It opposed both international economic sanctions and U.S. military action against Iraq. Articles on Iraq are available on its website.

Hoover Institution
Stanford University, Stanford, CA 94305-6010
(650) 723-1754 • fax: (650) 723-1687
website: www.hoover.stanford.edu

The Hoover Institution is a public policy research center devoted to advanced study of politics, economics, and political economy—both domestic and foreign—as well as international affairs. It publishes the quarterly *Hoover Digest*—which often includes articles on Iraq, the Middle East, and the war on terrorism—as well as a newsletter and special reports.

The Iraq Foundation
1012 Fourteenth St. NW, Suite 1110, Washington, DC 20005
(202) 347-4662 • fax: (202) 347-7897 / 7898
e-mail: iraq@iraqfoundation.org
website: www.iraqfoundation.org

The Iraq Foundation is a nonprofit, nongovernmental organization working for democracy and human rights in Iraq, and for a better international understanding of Iraq's potential as a contributor to political stability and economic progress in the Middle

East. Information on its projects as well as other information on Iraq can be found on its website.

Middle East Forum
1500 Walnut St., Suite 1050, Philadelphia, PA 19102
(215) 546-5406 • fax: (215) 546-5409
e-mail: info@meforum.org • website: www.meforum.org

The Middle East Forum is a think tank that works to define and promote American interests in Iraq and other parts of the Middle East. It supports strong American ties with Israel, Turkey, and other democracies as they emerge. It publishes the *Middle East Quarterly*, a policy-oriented journal. Its website includes articles on Iraq and other topics as well as a discussion forum.

Middle East Media Research Institute (MEMRI)
PO Box 27837, Washington, DC 20038-7837
(202) 955-9070 • fax: (202) 955-9077
e-mail: memri@memri.org • website: www.memri.org

MEMRI translates and disseminates articles and commentaries from Middle East media sources and provides analysis on the political, ideological, intellectual, social, cultural, and religious trends in the region.

Middle East Policy Council
1730 M St. NW, Suite 512, Washington, DC 20036-4505
(202) 296-6767 • fax: (202) 296-5791
e-mail: info@mepc.org • website: www.mepc.org

The Middle East Policy Council was founded in 1981 to expand public discussion and understanding of issues affecting U.S. policy in the Middle East. The council is a nonprofit educational organization that operates nationwide. Articles on Iraq can be found in the *Middle East Policy Journal*, its quarterly publication, and on its website.

Middle East Research and Information Project (MERIP)
1500 Massachusetts Ave. NW, Washington, DC 20005
(202) 223-3677 • fax: (202) 223-3604
website: www.merip.org

MERIP is a nonprofit, nongovernmental organization with no links to any religious, educational, or political organizations in the United States or elsewhere. Its mission is to educate the public about the contemporary Middle East with particular emphasis on U.S. foreign policy, human rights, and social justice issues. It publishes the bimonthly *Middle East Report.* Other publications include *Why Another War? A Backgrounder on the Iraq Crisis.*

U.S. Department of State
Bureau of Near Eastern Affairs
2201 C St. NW, Washington, DC 20520
(202) 647-4000
website: www.state.gov

The bureau deals with U.S. foreign policy and U.S. relations with the countries in the Middle East, including Iraq. Its website offers country information as well as news briefings and press statements on U.S. foreign policy.

Washington Institute for Near East Policy
1828 L St. NW, Suite 1050, Washington, DC 20036
(202) 452-0650 • fax: (202) 223-5364
e-mail: info@washingtoninstitute.org
website: www.washingtoninstitute.org

The institute is an independent, nonprofit research organization that provides information and analysis on the Middle East and U.S. policy in the region. It publishes numerous books including *How to Build a New Iraq After Saddam,* as well as policy papers and reports on regional politics, security, and economics. Its website includes a special "Focus on Iraq" section that features articles and reports in that nation.

Bibliography of Books

Amatzia Baram — *Between Impediment and Advantage: Saddam's Iraq.* Washington, DC: United States Institute of Peace, 1998.

Yossef Bodansky — *The High Cost of Peace: How Washington's Middle East Policy Left America Vulnerable to Terrorism.* Roseville, CA: Prima, 2002.

Joseph Braude — *The New Iraq: Rebuilding the Country for Its People, the Middle East, and the World.* New York: Basic Books, 2003.

Richard Butler and James C. Roy — *The Greatest Threat: Iraq, Weapons of Mass Destruction, and the Crisis of Global Security.* New York: Public Affairs, 2001.

Patrick Clawson, ed. — *How to Build a New Iraq After Saddam.* Washington, DC: Washington Institute for Near East Policy, 2002.

Toby Dodge and Steven Simon, eds. — *Iraq at the Crossroads: State and Society in the Shadow of Regime Change.* New York: Oxford University Press, 2003.

John L. Esposito and John O. Voll, eds. — *Islam and Democracy.* New York: Oxford University Press, 1996.

Deborah J. Gerner, ed. — *Understanding the Contemporary Middle East.* Boulder, CO: Lynne Reinner, 2000.

Khider Hamza — *Saddam's Bombmaker: The Daring Escape of the Man Who Built Iraq's Secret Weapon.* New York: Touchstone Books, 2001.

Dilip Hiro — *Iraq: In the Eye of the Storm.* New York: Thunder's Mouth Press, 2002.

Dilip Hiro — *Neighbors, Not Friends: Iraq and Iran After the Gulf Wars.* New York: Routledge, 2001.

Christopher Hitchens — *A Long Short War: The Postponed Liberation of Iraq.* New York: Plume, 2003.

Albert Hourani — *A History of the Arab Peoples.* Boston: Harvard University Press, 1997.

Lawrence F. Kaplan and William Kristol — *The War over Iraq: Saddam's Tyranny and America's Mission.* San Francisco: Encounter Books, 2003.

Martin Kramer — *Ivory Towers on Sand.* Washington, DC: Washington Institute for Near East Policy, 2001.

David W. Lesch, ed. — *The Middle East and the United States: A Historical and Political Reassessment.* Boulder, CO: Westview, 2003.

Bernard Lewis

What Went Wrong: The Clash Between Islam and Modernity in the Middle East. New York: HarperPerennial, 2003.

Sandra Mackey

The Reckoning: Iraq and the Legacy of Saddam Hussein. New York: W.W. Norton, 2002.

Norman Mailer

Why Are We at War? New York: Random House, 2003.

Kananis Makiya

Republic of Fear: The Politics of Modern Iraq. Revised edition. Berkeley and Los Angeles: University of California Press, 1998.

Debra A. Miller

Iraq. San Diego: Greenhaven Press, 2003.

Kenneth M. Pollack

The Threatening Storm: The Case for Invading Iraq. New York: Random House, 2002.

Milan Rai

War Plan Iraq: Ten Reasons Against War with Iraq. New York: Verso, 2002.

Scott Ritter

Endgame: Solving the Iraq Crisis. New York: Simon & Schuster, 2002.

Micah L. Sifry and Christopher Cerf, eds.

The Iraq War Reader: History, Documents, Opinions. New York: Touchstone Books, 2003.

Daniel Silverfarb

Britain's Informal Empire in the Middle East: A Case Study of Iraq, 1929–1941. Oxford, UK: Oxford University Press, 1997.

Norman Solomon et al.

Target Iraq: What the News Media Didn't Tell You. New York: Context Books, 2003.

Charles Tripp

History of Modern Iraq. 2nd edition. Cambridge, MA: Cambridge University Press, 2002.

Harlan Ullman

Unfinished Business: Afghanistan, the Middle East, and Beyond—Defusing the Dangers That Threaten American Security. New York: Citadel Press, 2002.

Index

demonstrate importance of complying with U.S., 74
not presented truthfully, 20, 45, 48
regime change and, 41
were advancement of American strategy, 48
Iraqi people supported, 37
Kurdish forces in, 148
length of, 19
U.S. responsibilities as result of, 81, 92
was justified
geopolitically
con, 29–30
national security
has decreased, 74, 75–76
was not threatened, 43, 48
will suffer, 30–31
was part of hegemonic designs of Bush, 69
weapons of mass destruction were not present, 45
will incite Islamic radicals, 40
will worsen situation in Middle East, 40
existence of weapons of mass destruction and, 54, 56
for global security, 19–20, 25–26, 61, 62
for national security, 22–24, 52, 65, 97
morally and ethically, 24–25, 34–35, 37, 38, 65–66, 67
con, 28–29, 30, 42–43
was validation of Bush Doctrine, 83
Islam
divisions in, 147
fundamentalists
Bush was unprepared for strength of, 49
have gained power, 49, 72–73, 116
Iraq War will strengthen, 29, 40
theocracy is goal of, 143
is only organized alternative to repression, 139
is way of life, 125, 138–40
must be integrated into government, 125–27
in Turkey, 140
see also Shiite Muslims; Sunni Muslims
Israel
is safer as result of Iraq War, 61, 62
Persian Gulf War and, 29
U.S. must support peace with Palestinians and, 76–77

Jefferson, Thomas, 152

Judis, John B., 48, 177

Kagan, Robert, 23
Kahn, Herman, 53
Karzai, Hamid, 87
Kennedy, John F., 77
Al Khafaji, Isam, 183
Khalilzad, Zalmay, 92
Kipper, Judith, 49
Kosovo, 86, 87, 98, 165–66
Krauthamer, Charles, 40
Kristof, Nicholas D., 86
Kristol, William, 23
Kubba, Laith, 132
Kucinich, Dennis, 30
Kurds
autonomous rule for, 122, 160
characteristics of, 147–48
under Hussein, 15, 34
independence for, 167–68
during Iraq War, 118
political parties representing, 135
Kurtz, Stanley, 97
Kuwait, 15

Lipset, Seymour Martin, 178

Macedonia, 87, 165–66
Mack, Andrew, 43
Mackey, Sandra, 148
Madere, Tom, 85
Madison, James, 161
Makiya, Kanan, 37, 41–42
Massing, Michael, 36
Maude, Stanley, 124
Meigs, Montgomery, 87
Middle East
democratic Iraq will be model for, 150, 151
Hussein was not major player in Israeli-Palestinian conflict of, 74
Iraq War will worsen situation in, 29–30, 40
con, 61, 62, 65
should be weapons of mass destruction–free zone, 76
United States and
must support peace in, 76–77
supports repressive regimes in, 71
Miller, Judith, 47
Muslims. See Islam; Shiite Muslims; Sunni Muslims
Myard, Jacques, 64

Nales, Jack, 88
Nasir, Awad, 99
National Security Strategy (NSS) of U.S., 58–59

200

al-Qaeda
Iraq has aided, 22
con, 69
Iraq War will detract from war
against, 30
is greatest threat to U.S., 39–40, 76
was not destroyed in Afghanistan, 87
Qasim, Abd Al Karim, 183

regime change
is real reason for Iraq War, 41
is responsibility of U.S. as global
leader, 23
justified Iraq War, 20, 34–35, 37, 38,
65–66, 67
was inevitable, 62
Republic of Fear (Makiya), 37
Rice, Condoleezza, 138
Ritter, Scott, 69
Rumsfeld, Donald
exit strategy of, 97
on imperialism, 95
mobile Armed Forces and, 83
on nation building, 152
on weapons of mass destruction, 46
Rushdie, Salman, 38
Russia, 20, 110–11
Ryan, Joan, 137

Saleh, Imad, 86
Salih, Barham, 118
Saudi Arabia, 75
Schelling, Thomas, 53
Schlesinger, Arthur, Jr., 41
Schrage, Michael, 51
Shiite Muslims
characteristics of, 147
fundamentalist clerics of, filled
power vacuum created by Iraq War,
49, 72–73
under Hussein, 15
Islamic theocracy is goal of, 116,
143, 160
uprising by, 34
Shinseki, Eric, 49, 83, 86, 87–88
Somalia, 98
South Korea, 184–85
Stanislaw, Joseph, 171
strategic deception, policy of, 52–56
Sullivan, Andrew, 54
Sunni Muslims, 147–48, 160, 166–67

Taheri, Amir, 101
Taiwan, 184–85
terrorists
fight against
American commitment to, 19–20,
59, 60

should be priority, 39–40
democratic Iraq will, 97
Iraq War and
furthered goals of, 73
will detract from war against, 30
will increase number of, 40, 105
will increase threat to U.S. from,
31
theocracy, 116, 143, 160
This Kind of War (Fehrenbach), 89
*Threatening Storm: The Case for
Invading Iraq, The* (Pollack), 38,
39–40
Tocqueville, Alexis de, 179
transition economies, 172, 173
Tripp, Charles, 182
Turkey
behavior of, during Iraq War, 167
Islam in, 126, 140
Kurds in, 148
strongman government in, 130
U.S. in postwar Iraq will antagonize,
101
will benefit from stable Iraq, 121–22
Tuwaitha Nuclear Research Center, 46

unipolar moment, 59
United Nations
Bush speech to, 61
economic sanctions imposed by,
15–16, 19
had disastrous effects, 70–71
should have been lifted, 43
Hussein showed contempt for, 63
weapons inspectors, 16, 20, 69
authorization for, 23, 24
defiance of, 61–62, 63
United States
aided Hussein, 70, 183
Armed Forces
in Afghanistan, 86, 87
in Bosnia, 85
in Kosovo, 86, 87
oil fields secured by, 71
reaction to, 101
democratic Iraq and, 97, 119–20,
142–43
has failed to live up to Fourth
Geneva Convention, 71
has responsibilities of global
leadership, 23
Iraqi distrust of, 70–72, 84, 129
is republic, not democracy, 142
Middle East and, 71, 76–77
national security of
has decreased, 74, 75–76
strategy for, 58–59
was not threatened, 43, 48